CONVERSATIONS WITH CASSANDRA

By Sister M. Madeleva, C.S.C.

Sister M. Madeleva, C.S.C.

CONVERSATIONS WITH CASSANDRA

Who Believes in Education?

THE MACMILLAN COMPANY

New York 1961

Nihil obstat:

James Egan, O.P.

Imprimatur:

✠ Leo A. Pursley, D.D.
Bishop of Fort Wayne-South Bend

May 1, 1961

First Printing

Permission has been granted for quotations from *The Collected Poems of
G. K. Chesterton*, Copyright 1932 by Dodd, Mead & Company, Inc.; *The Little
Prince* by Antoine de Saint-Exupéry, Harcourt, Brace and Company, Inc.;
A Rime of the Rood by Charles O'Donnell, C.S.C., Longmans, Green & Co.,
Inc.; *Marcelino* by Sanchez-Silva, The Newman Press; *A Sleep of Prisoners*
and *The Dark Is Light Enough* by Christopher Fry, Oxford University Press,
Inc.; *Gift from the Sea* by Anne Morrow Lindbergh, Pantheon Books, Inc.;
"Second April" by Edna St. Vincent Millay, from *Collected Poems*, Harper
and Brothers, Copyright 1921–1948 by Edna St. Vincent Millay, by permission
of Norma Millay Ellis.
The chapter entitled "Dame Julian of Norwich" first appeared in *The
Image of the Work*, published by the University of California Press.

The Macmillan Company, New York
Brett-Macmillan Ltd., Galt, Ontario

Printed in the United States of America

Library of Congress catalog card number: 61-12189

To
Aunt Alice
with gratitude and love

Preface

"EDUCATION" is a militant, a closely constructed military word. The business of "leading out" almost immediately suggests an army, with or without banners.

Every teacher of genuine dimensions subscribes to the militancy of his vocation. He relies on its military regimes and disciplines. He is well aware of the panoply and display of banners. These may be terrific—to fall into the vernacular; they may be terrifying—to face facts.

Over the past half century he may recall a number of them: the elective system, accrediting agencies, standardization, specialization, progressive education, the Great Books, the call of the sciences, audiovisual aids, airborne education, teaching machines, propagandas unlimited. Teachers, students, and schools have experienced all these and are still rational. We are said to be secure when we can stand everything that can happen to us. If this is the test we are on a fair way to security in education.

This may be the moment for Cassandra to speak. It may be time for her to tell us that we have not met or solved our big problems, that we have not even guessed or dreamed them. As prophetess she sees our world in its suddenly expanded horizons, in its terrifying frontiers, in its newly revealed infinitudes. She believes in the possibilities of and for this world and for us, its contemporary inhabitants. She believes in education in tremendous dimensions.

Cassandra is by natural endowment a person of faith. Cassandra is every teacher of vision, of daring, of great desires. There are regiments of these in our country, in our world today.

We have said that "education" is a military word, a term to call up national defenses. Armies are composed of soldiers and officers. I am calling the officers. I am enlisting our Cassandras who share the faith in education for a new earth and a new heaven.

Reciprocally, I am asking the exploding armies of students to look for, to ask for, to follow these officers, these teachers. Youth is torn today between security and service. I ask the great army of intelligent youth to prick their iridescent bubbles of security and to find them to be only bubbles. Service is their banner, their blueprint of being, their active education.

Here we are, Cassandra, teachers and students, who share in at least some of your belief, your vision, your faith. Let us talk of these together. Let us find with you not only present ends but new beginnings for our militant and military enterprise.

S. M. M.

Contents

Contents

I

Cassandra Speaks on Education

CASSANDRA was a most unhappy girl. Of all the earmarked children of Priam she was the most dubiously gifted. The gods had endowed her with a knowledge of the future with the foil that no one would believe her. A prophet in ill-fated Troy, she and her foreknowledge were repudiated. Troy refused to believe the preposterous and disturbing predictions of this half-mad girl.

She belongs to a distinguished, a rejected, but an unfrustrated company. Who of us has forgotten from high school classes the ominous mandate, "Carthage must be destroyed," or the grim warning, "Beware the ides of March." Fewer of us realize that four major and twelve minor books of the Old Testament are books of prophecy relating to God's chosen people. The significant thing to be remembered is not that these prophets were ignored, persecuted, thrown into pits and lions' dens, sawed in two. The important fact to be kept in mind is that their prophecies, while foretelling immediate disaster, were followed by purgation, their repentance consequent on purification.

All prophets are teachers. They are lovers of the children of men and prepared to die for any or every generation of them. They are all Cassandras. In this hour, Cassandra may well speak of education.

Alan Moorehead, the Australian author, journalist, war correspondent, contributed to the September, 1960, number of *Horizon* a leading article on *The Coming of the White Man*. Let me quote his three opening sentences:

"To every distant shore, some time in the last five hundred years, the light-skinned stranger came, bearing Western civilization. His image, seen by native artists, was scratched on rock, carved in wood, woven in cloth, or painted on paper. Now, as the tide of white expansion ebbs, this graphic record remains to mark a fateful moment in the history of world culture."

All but one dependent clause is commentary on the past. This clause looks to the future. This is Cassandra's business. The clause is: "Now, as the tide of white expansion ebbs."

We are in that ebbing tide, have been in it long enough now to observe receding shore lines, tidal, often primitive influxes into areas but recently vacated by us, by the white man. Tides such as this are controlled by the moons of basic human needs, ambitions, growth, and expansion of peoples, racial and national unrest, adventure, discovery, exploitation, the Christian mandate to go into the entire world and preach the gospel, the Moslem mandate; the kingdom of heaven lies in the shadow of the crossing of swords, the Communist mandate of world revolution. Not one of these currents is absent from the tides moving worlds and peoples and boundaries today. History can give us only relative help in computing the duration of their ebb. They will come to an absolute low by the very laws that move them. Then what?

With the withdrawal of white leaderships and ownerships in the great undeveloped areas of Asia and Africa, and with the development of a middle class among the peoples themselves, an era of self-determination is imminent. The white man has had experience in such re-formations. He has the responsibility to teach these young nations, these emerging governments, by example, by practical help, by noninterference, by love. His technique should be the technique of transformation, transfiguration. Peoples do not have to be destroyed in order to be saved. Races do not have to be embittered in order to be effective. Civilization is not the lifting of men out of the conditions of primitive savagery into the savageries of annihilation or worse. We cannot be obtuse to our responsibilities. We cannot be lethargic. We cannot be indifferent. We are our brother's keepers and all humanity is in that brotherhood. We haven't a single right to any prestige that the white man enjoys or has ever enjoyed or may hope for unless we are actually accepting and fulfilling our part in its tremendous responsibilities.

Bigness and firstness are not our peculiar mission to mankind. They may be bad cases of political astigmatism. They may be dust thrown in our eyes by propaganda. For the moment, they have us hypnotized and deluded. Of what values are bigness and firstness in the areas in which we pursue them so madly? Have we ever asked the question calmly and answered it sanely? They can become chimeras leading us into pursuits futile if not fatal, expending our best resources to no ends better than pride frustrated or fulfilled. Both are frightful states of a nation's mind.

Or if we persist in being the biggest and the first, let it be in Christianity, in the universality of brotherly love. Our absolute greatness lies in keeping faith in God alive in an apostatizing world. This is a mission of holiness.

Many things we need never try to do or to be. Other peoples have their areas of preeminence also. We can teach truth; we can teach the dignity of man, the basic equality of all men, their brotherhood as sons of God, the loving fatherhood of God.

The white man has done this before. He must do it again, and always until time itself runs out. This vocation came to

Saint Paul at Troas in Asia Minor. The Western world in the person of a Macedonian appealed to him, "Come over into Macedonia and help us." Paul understood that God had called him to preach the gospel to the Western world. We are still the Western world. We still have this gift for men.

By the year 400 A.D. the apparently impossible had happened in Europe. A small minority of Christians had replaced the invincible pagan power of the Roman Empire. There came such a cyclic ebb and flow of ethnic, racial power forces as we are in today. Waves of Eastern peoples, Visigoths, Ostrogoths, moved across the Roman provinces from Western Asia to the Atlantic. Cultures had to recede before them. Reevaluations had to be made quickly, historically speaking. The Vandals took a longer way round and came up to Rome from Northern Africa. The Northman took a longer time and came into France somewhat later, as did the Angles and Saxons to Roman Britain. Even so, the latter gave the world the name of one brave country, England.

We are considering tidal waves of peoples earlier than the one of which we are now a part. The great migrations from the third to the sixth century are instructive for us in retrospect. Cassandra would have needed no gift of prophecy to draw from them omens and auspices for our future.

The barbarian invasions were literally a wading into existing countries, peoples, homes, lives, civilizations. They have given to our language two of our ugliest words, "vandalism" and "Hun." But they have contributed two of our noblest forms of architecture, the Norman castle, the Gothic cathedral.

They were halted outside Paris by a young girl, Geneviève, with the great human gifts of food and drink. What a precedent for us! She is now a patron saint of the city and of all France. They were turned back, these barbarians, from the gate of Rome by the faith and courage of Pope Leo I. Diverted in their progress as the scourge of God, they gradually became Christians, at times through mass baptisms. Within a century the children of these pagan barbarians were Christian saints. This integration and assimilation of barbarian with civilized peoples formed the core, the red blood, the tough resilient fiber of our Western world.

By what processes of assimilation, integration, and formation did all this happen? Not by the backwash of the Roman Empire, nor the adaptation of the proud legacy of Roman law. It came about by the heroic work of the Christian missionaries and the equally heroic work of the Christian schools. As these Eastern tribes relocated west of the Danube and west of the Oder they reformed their lives and were reformed spiritually by Christian missionaries.

One of the earliest translations of the Bible was into East Gothic. Ulfilas and his sturdy brother monks did not begin by teaching the Goths Latin. They learned the speech of the Goths, invented an alphabet for them, and put the scriptures into the newly-formed written language of these people. Echelons of great men went then, as they are doing now, to tell these young Europeans-in-the-making the great world news of Christianity.

Integrated with all the apostles of the nations were the Benedictine monks, the fathers of education in the West. The academic curriculum as we know it today owes its beginnings to Saint Benedict, the father of Western monasticism. By the end of those restive two centuries of migration and relocation, tens of thousands of so-called barbarians had become Christians, had become Europeans, had become the parents of Western civilization, the sponsors of our own Christian culture.

What had become of the Roman Empire in the process? What of the first three centuries of the Christian era in Western Europe? Had they been destroyed, discredited, annihilated? Looking back, we see how they all fed into that great growing, living, moving Western world from which most of us, our national life, our culture have come.

Even to Cassandra the present picture is not too bleak, the future is not too disturbing. Indeed, if we are in our right minds, it need not be disturbing at all. It can simply be the opportunity of greatest magnitude that Christian civilization and Christian culture have ever had of demonstrating their validity, their feasibility to produce peace on earth and good will to men.

During our first hundred years of national life our Founding Fathers came to these shores for religious freedom. They came to worship God and to worship Him freely. They built churches, houses for Him. They built schools, Christian schools to house the intellectual life of their children, of our first Americans. These are our bases of existence. These are our unique gifts to all men, to one world. The pattern of European ancestry repeated itself then. It will repeat itself again in this age of world ebb and flood tides. The Christian faith and the Christian schools are ours to preserve, ours to give to all nations, all people. They are the white man's constant shore line in humanity's ebb and flow. They are a shore line for all the world.

We are Christians. We are teachers. We are students. We are not crying out futilely to an incredulous world. We are not prophets of inevitable defeat and possible annihilation. Cassandra of today speaks the language of the Christian. She assumes that we as Christians understand, accept, and fulfill our responsibilities in their totality. She foresees that we will receive and assimilate the peoples and their cultures that our shifting worlds are bringing to us. She assumes that as teachers and students we will repeat the pattern of the early Christian missionaries, the Benedictine schools. She fully expects us to salvage from the topless towers of our many babels, the confusion of our many contemporary blasphemous tongues, the Decalogue, the Lord's Prayer, the Beatitudes. She looks to us to herald them in pentecostal tongues, to release them to the power of every wind of the Holy Spirit that shakes our world today. They are her prophecy and ours against the crescent and the sickle. They are her sign, our labarum that we will give God a chance, that we will make Christianity come resplendently true.

II

The Beginning of Work

As a prefatory note to their joint autobiography Rose Hawthorne Lathrop and her husband Julian wrote, "The end of
writing, the beginning of work." For them writing had been
a fine art in the literary tradition of Rose's father, Nathaniel
Hawthorne. It terminated as such with her conversion to
Catholicism and was readapted to the apostolate of the
Church.

Later, as you will remember, Rose founded the Servants
for Relief of Incurable Cancer in New York City and spent
her life caring for these incurable patients in the great hospital which she succeeded in having erected. This was the
beginning of work in heroic dimensions.

There is an aptness in this example in our present consideration of college education, particularly the education of
women. The program is a process of study, a four-year intellectual experience before the beginning of a life of work.
We all know what the content of these years of study must
include. We can have only natural or inspired guesses on
years of work to come which will be your lives.

Herbert Hoover remembers how, as a child, he was sent
regularly to attend Sabbath day Quaker meetings. There was

little a boy could do about the enveloping silence of those
meetings, he decided, except to count his toes. Occasionally
the spirit moved his Aunt Hannah to arise and say that she
was going to speak her mind. With or without the counting
of toes, this seems an opportune time for a college president
to speak her mind.

Let us begin with three definitions. College is a life four
years long, completely blueprinted, with guides, guidance,
instruction, sanctions, every step of the way, and commensu-
rate rewards at the end. These are the four top years of life
for every one of you, decisive, unforgettable, highly condensed,
most concrete. They are your capacity years.

Your intellectual program may often seem to be too pre-
occupied with matters only remotely related to the lived life
of the student, either while at college or after. How does one
reconcile sixteen hours of theology, fifteen of philosophy,
eight of laboratory science with the problems immediately
confronting the college graduate: the job, the wedding, the
year abroad, the career, the vocation, the avocation, with all
their mutations. But these same intransigents emanating
from the dean's office and looking the student squarely in the
face from the pages of the college bulletin are the very making
of her, as vital as air and sleep and water to her becoming a
person with a trained, healthy, normal mind.

College is a city, an intellectual trailer home. Though the
connotations may seem to lack dignity, the bases of comparison are entirely worthy. Life in America, being what it is
today, the analogy cannot be repugnant. It assumes horizons
international, social exchanges and amenities as wide and as
welcome, opportunities for change and variety so dear to the
restless American heart. Yet, for all the impermanence of the
college city, it carries a basic permanence that inheres in no
other four years of the college graduate's life. Who among
us, however stoic in temperament, can set at naught the bona
fide thrill of getting back to one's college campus? Though

the word itself, *campus,* means a camp, a stopping place, it involves some of our deepest roots.

We may not have been back to our college for a quarter of a century. We may not meet a person who knows us or whom we know. The plant may have outgrown all our memories. But we never know our latent capacities for a peculiar and valid sentiment of loyalty to Alma Mater until we go back to college, this trailer city of our minds.

If this is true of the campus, the buildings, what shall be said of that fourth order of humanity, our schoolmates? But here I must put a limit to speaking my mind. You will all want to speak yours, sooner or later, on this perennial, delicious subject.

College is a space world for a space age, a world of metaphysical rockets, jets, satellites. During four years the college takes its students into the world of intellectual space, into ballistic exploration of deep space. How often in her courses in theology or philosophy or science, has the student's mind been projected beyond the farthest sun, into the Infinity in which we live and move and have our being? How many have brought back communicable records from such projections? Our Courier, our Discoverer, our Echo are slow-moving imitators of the majestic speed and instancy with which our minds reach deep into outer space and report back from infinity in the intellectual order. Do not think that this space age is foreign to us. It is our promised land, our homeland. Infinity is our proper dimension.

Having defined college in good round terms, let us fit ourselves into it. This means fitting ourselves for work, a bilateral activity. Let us be frank and direct in our statements. As students you do not demand enough work of your teachers. You do not begin to ask from them all that they have and want to give you. They are much brighter than you may think they are. You do not make their lessons hard enough. You do not keep them busy keeping up with you. They represent a very large, rich, ballistic world. Use them as ballistic stations from which the mysteries of knowledge and the knowledge of mysteries can be radioed back, telephoned back, bounced back to you.

Use them as friends. In four years, or sooner, the academic distinction of teacher and student will no longer exist. Anticipate that happy day of "lackademic" freedom. Put down deep roots in this common ground of common allegiances to the best values and the best years of your lives.

We must not forget that we are engaged in a bilateral activity. We teachers have our homework, too. Chronically, we underestimate you, your intelligence, your generosity, your willingness to work, even your willingness to sacrifice, to give up, to do without. We do not give you objectives big enough, assignments hard enough, motives exalted enough. The Dean's list is one-dimensional. It is the least we can ask. Add a second, a third, a fourth dimension in richness of readings, art perceptions, versatility, the qualities of mercy, the sublimated arts of friendship. Never again, and nowhere else will you be so surrounded with opportunities for all these. They are assignments that we your teachers must ask of you.

Inevitably we will make the mistake of overestimating your experience. We will half expect you to see things from our maturer point of view. Take this as a compliment and grow up to it. You can. These preparations, this beginning of work will ask for everything you are or can be. It is only four years off for the youngest of you, hard years. There are no easy ways.

What can we do together? We can work together, pray together, play together, all of us as adults. Your years of adolescence are past. Swallow hard, but face this fact. You are no longer children. You are maturing young women. What does this mean for you? Let me tell you in the words of George Shuster, recently retired president of Hunter College: "I lived," he said, "in Poitiers as a student in a room

looking out on the old street up which Jeanne d'Arc had come
to see the Dauphin. Like many a soldier just out of the
trenches, I thought of the place I had to make for myself in
the world rather than of how I would go about it or why.
Early one morning I overheard two girls talking on their
way to work. 'As for myself, I want to do my work well . . .
and to die well,' I heard one say. . . . To want to do one's
work well. . . .

"Mortality's best prelude to immortality would be to find
nothing in life of which one had to be terribly ashamed. . . .
In the conversation of the two French girls I found the conviction that life must retain a quality only the word holiness
can describe."

We have no alternative. We will do our work and we will
do that work well. In its unique diversities, all of our work
must, I think, focus today on one subject. We have drawn
analogies from our space age. We must descend to the devastating ideologies of communism. This is the philosophical,
sociological climate with which your future will be surrounded. There is little more important that your college
can teach you, even for survival, than a thorough, working
understanding of this menace to the modern world. I might
quote for you from an ominous address of Dr. Charles Malik.
He says: "The deepest crisis of the west is the crisis of faith
in its own values. . . . A civilization is doomed if it is not
creatively conscious of something universal and human it can
and must give. . . . The civilization at whose heart pulsate
Aristotle and Aquinas and Dante and Shakespeare and Lincoln, the civilization which has been blessed and transformed
by Christ needs only a mighty hand to shake it out of its
slumber and once shaken . . . there is nothing it cannot
dare and do."

I might cite the panoramic survey of the English historian,
Hugh Seton-Watson who, in his book, *Neither War nor
Peace,* offers the devastating alternatives, "Either the peoples

must accept more discomfort . . . or they risk being forced to decide between mass suicide and capitulation to the enemy. 'A high standard of living is the first priority' is just not true. To be alive and not to be a slave is more important than to live opulently." This must be an end of our study, a major office and an uncompromising beginning of our work. Our own Allen W. Dulles, director of Central Intelligence, made our assignment unmistakable in an article in the *United States News and World Report*.

"We need far and wide in this country more education on the whole history of the Communistic movement. . . . By and large, however, except in the graduate field, or in specialized schools and seminars, these subjects are not generally taught. . . . Our students are not yet afforded a broad opportunity to gain the essential background knowledge of Communist history and policy. And we should start this education in our secondary schools. . . . We should not be afraid to teach the subject. A history of Communism and all its work would bear its own indictment of the system. Let the facts speak for themselves. . . . During the years immediately ahead it seems more likely that the immediate danger we will be facing, and on a worldwide basis, will be Communist political, economic and subversive action and penetration; not a hot or nuclear war."

Are we blind? If so, how blind are we to the ideologies that surround us, closing in on us? Will the inevitable happen to us? Shall we, too, find ourselves strangled by this octopus that has reached out within the past decade to the whole world?

Mr. Seton-Watson has said: "A high standard of living is not the first priority. . . . To be alive and not to be a slave is more important than to live opulently." This means a willingness to accept discomfort; it means the actual acceptance of discomfort. It means that we do not need two cars in every garage, a telephone, a TV in practically every room, a mink coat or stole for every mother and daughter, a swimming pool in every yard, or at least in every motel. Our excess in luxuries, in multitudes of expendables has scandalized the world, has branded us as a play nation with all its pagan and effeminate implications, has reduced us to softness, unwilling to accept, much less to seek sacrifice, and to endure it if forced upon us.

Have our magic for invention, our genius for finding easy ways, our resulting opulence poisoned us into a gangrened and bloated generation? If so, we can lose no time in applying the best existing antibiotics to check and to destroy these deadly germs. These antibiotics are sacrifice, courage, uncompromising loyalty and allegiance to our country, its laws, its leaders, heroic love of God and His will, and a lifetime of prayer. All of these can be set in their proper places and order among us. Our colleges can be not only the capital health spots of national life in our country. They can become a *spes unica,* the hope of the world.

The ominous panorama we have just reviewed blueprints two objectives for all of us: the end or the ends of study; the beginning of work. If, as Dr. Malik has said, the great crisis of the West is the crisis of faith in its own values, we must direct our study to the establishment or reestablishment of this faith. We must discover the continent that we call ours, the country that we call our country, the land of America and its United States that are ours, peculiarly ours. What do we know about these that makes them worth living for, worth dying for? We can ask these questions of our men in service, men who are trained to die for the great freedoms that we know to be holy. I am asking you who are women.

The universal symbol of America to all the world is not a flag, a skyscraper, a bomber, a satellite; it is a woman. It is the Statue of Liberty in New York harbor. This majestic woman lifts her torch into the skies of our country, a home with the hopes and the sanctities of freedom to everyone watching the horizon for the first sight of our shores. The thousands returning from abroad she welcomes home. To the tens of thousands coming as immigrants she is the symbolic mother of a promised land. To all of us going abroad, year after year, she is our most concrete symbol of a great nation. We remember that this nation is dedicated to another woman, Mary Immaculate.

The womanhood of America must assume its proper role to the peoples in quest of freedom if, by chance, freedom still exists for them anywhere. This means that we must begin at once to practice sacrifice, to do without our scandalous unessentials in order that others may know the minimums for mere existence. It means that we must define and understand such ideas as liberty, freedom, human rights in order that we may apply them perfectly and constantly. It means that we will astonish the world and ourselves by being Christians.

Our study for the year, our work for a lifetime must advert particularly to another field of insidious infection. This is the area or areas of mental health. Our conversations, our idioms, our recreations, our pictures and radio programs are saturated with quackeries on mental health. We can scarcely be considered normal unless we have at least one complex. This begins with a child's protest against spinach and continues through a wilderness of likes and dislikes that used to keep us normal. Now they categorize us into some of a possible million abnormalities.

This slow, steady subversion of our healthy American people, particularly our boys and girls, into subdivisions of the subnormal and the abnormal is the most horrifyingly diseased form of propaganda to which we are being exposed at this moment. If enough of us can suspect or be convinced that we have a complex, that is, that we are not quite normal, the sanity of our nation is under question, under attack. Let us declare an embargo against complexes. Let us boycott them, the pictures, the programs, the literature that peddles them. Let us refuse to be host to them as we would to lice or unmentionable diseases.

I am not talking about careful and expert care of our health in all its aspects, physical, mental, moral, spiritual. I am talking of the spurious and poisonous invasions of our life and our world by the most subversive of all communistic techniques.

We are speaking about the end of study, the beginning of work. We have cited the young girl of Poitiers and her simple composite of life, "I want to do my work well . . . and to die well." We quoted George Shuster's comment on this statement, his conviction that to do one's work well and to die well, "life must retain a quality only the word *holiness* can describe." Here we are, a happy, healthy, earnest, enthusiastic world of teachers and students, possessing the greatest goods, facing the greatest evils men have ever known. How are we going to apply our intelligence, our resources, our graces, natural and supernatural, to proper solutions? What kind of students will we be? What kind of teachers? What kind of Christians? How shall we do our work? How near shall we approach to holiness?

III

Why Do We Educate Our Daughters?

In ASKING and attempting to answer the question, "Why do we educate our daughters?" we must examine three antecedent questions and their answers.

The first is: Shall we educate our daughters? This question is not obsolete. It is asked more often than one might think. The history of American education for the past century and a half provides abundant and impressive answers. The historic female colleges, the exclusive academies and seminaries for young ladies, the cautiously opened doors of state universities, the daring hazards of coeducation, the graduate and professional schools are successive answers. The percentage of girls in college today is an additional reply. They average over 40 per cent of our college and university population. The place and status of highly qualified women on our college and university faculties are also significant.

As yet, full professional status, rank and salary are granted only to exceptional women. Those non-coeducational universities, the last strongholds for men in the American college system, do not invite women to their faculties. Here, possibly, discretion is the better part of both valor and value.

Past and present stand in affirmative answer to our question, "Shall we educate our daughters?" Yes, we shall.

The second question is: "Can we educate our daughters?"
The answer is not as easy as one might imagine. Money is
not the answer. Scholarship is not the answer, nor prestige,
nor pressure.

Our ability to educate our daughters depends on the essence of education itself and on the combined power of college and student to come into the possession of this rare essence. Indeed, it is not unlike a perfume, a distillation of the
rich and beautiful and holy flowering of the human mind
since the birth of thought. It is, in its best beginnings and its
perfect end, the gravitation of man to truth that is God, and
the quest of man by God through truth and beauty and
goodness. Can our daughters move irrevocably into these
areas? Can they assimilate this essence of education?

Against such a quest, such natural and supernatural gravitation to the perfections of their minds are ranged the bewildering impacts of the day and of their particular generation. Shall we particularize? Shall we enumerate?

Secularism stands first and conditions all that follows. We
call this the Christian era. Our history moves in the year of
our Lord, *anno Domini*. We identify ours as a Christian
civilization, as contrasted with the Moslem, the Oriental, the
African cultures. Yet nowhere, except perhaps setting Sun-
day apart from our work-a-day week, does our world move
deliberately and intentionally in patterns of love or faith in
God. Its attitudes, when not indifferent, are antagonistic or
hostile to religious belief. Can we teach our daughters to
live complete, happy, holy lives in a world that adores itself?
This idolatry sets up altars to a multitude of false gods inviting their worship. Standardization is the most ubiquitous.

Standardizations in all areas and on every level tend to
dominate their learning, their living. They look at and listen
to the same vapidities, the worst as well as the best that celluloid has to offer. They are pressured to look, not like themselves, but like pitiful parodies of the motion picture deities

of the moment. One need not elaborate. Against standardization from lipstick to leotards, the college girl today must fight the difficult fight of keeping her independence, of being simply and completely herself.

She must battle for personal identity and freedom against the gregarious disease of togetherness. She finds herself at the mysterious frontier of existence, the undiscovered country of her own potential womanhood. This she must cross alone. For it she needs courage and a quality of reverence new to her. But the human mind loves mystery. She will find herself divided between bewilderment and wonder in the world of her own youth. All of this she cannot explore against a background of crowds or the cacophonies of the air. Hamlet's problem, "to be, or not to be" recurs to her in a desperation of instinctive demands to be herself.

If standardization is a tyranny, security is an obsession. With their parents and their teachers, our daughters share a passion for security. Social life is bound round with such companionship as will save one from being alone or dependent on one's own social expedients for a moment. Our generation has not realized that "security is mortal's chiefest enemy." This trap the devil, in the persons of the three witches, laid for Macbeth to lure him into an orgy of murders, ending in his own.

We must educate our daughters to the fact that we are secure only when we can stand everything that can happen to us. We must teach them to incorporate this kind of security into every day of their lives. They will thank us for the lesson. They will come to a place of courage and peace that the most carefully devised insurance cannot procure for them.

We teachers and parents have cause to ask "Can we educate our daughters?" Can we teach them the power of their own inviolable being, the invincible strength of their goodness and beauty? Can we say to them what Coventry Patmore said more than a century ago?

Ah, wasteful woman! she who may
　On her sweet self set her own price,
Knowing he cannot choose but pay,
　How has she cheapen'd paradise!
How given for nought her priceless gift,
　How spoiled the bread and spilled the wine,
Which, spent with due respective thrift,
　Had made brutes men and men divine!

Can we educate these beautiful girls in the fortitude of the valiant woman?

Our third question is: "Do we educate our daughters? Do we teach them? If so, what?"

A few weeks ago two of our teachers went to the home of one of our alumnae for a committee meeting. The children had been waiting the day long for their arrival. When they finally came, late in the afternoon, the impatient four-year-old greeted them, "Why are you so late? Where were you?" The sisters, happy at being awaited with so much eagerness, answered, "We have been at school. You see, we teach." To which came the child's impatient reply, "I don't know teach. But Sisters, what's in a bomb?" How many of us wish we knew or could guess what's in the bomb of education today and tomorrow! Twenty-five years ago debating teams at Oxford met on the subject: "Resolved: that it would be better if America had not been discovered." In late January of this year (1960), twelve hundred undergraduates packed the hall of the Oxford University Union Society to listen to the debate teams battle the subject: "Resolved: that this house holds America responsible for the spreading vulgarity in Western society." Stereotyped United States culture, mass reduction of human dignity, liquors, and the selling of sex were cited to support the resolution.

This is one close-up of our American college-bred world from overseas. One need not point out the place of our daughters in the picture. In a quarter of a century, their education has not bettered the impression of America on the European mind.

Our caravans of tourists do little to improve the picture. Many shrines in Canada and Europe find it necessary to post very specific signs forbidding women to enter insufficiently clad. Anyone visiting Saint Peter's in the summer remembers the intransigent double guard at every door of the basilica. Their duty is to require women to cover their arms and shoulders before entering. The American girl and the American woman outnumber all other groups to come under correction. These examples and these records are not pleasant. Thousands of these tourists are college students. Do we educate our daughters?

Oxford mock-debates and sweaters at the doors of Saint Peter's are certainly not the final tests of the education of the American girl or of our ability to educate her. They are but straws, but none of us is proud or pleased with their indication of the way the winds are blowing.

We come to our final question, "Why do we educate our daughters?" Briefly, we educate them for exactly the reason for which God made them: to know, to love, to serve, to glorify Him now and forever. To achieve this we use the avenues proper to education, the avenues of their minds.

This does not mean that they are all to be theologians or philosophers, or that they are all to dedicate their lives as religious teachers or as religious women. They will do and be something of all these.

But in consequence of their education they know God through the major work of which they have experience, His world, His universe. Through their years at college they have tried to understand, with reverence, the cumulative and unfolding patterns of existence through the cultures, the sciences, the histories, the arts of peoples. They have penetrated with intellectual excitement into the profundities of the sim-

ple injunctions, "Just think!" and "Let me be." They have
moved from the contingencies of being in which we live
to the absolute simplicity of being that is God. The astound-
ing intuitions of a child, the ominous awakenings of primitive
peoples, the unimaginable magnitudes of outer space are all
proper to their world and parts of their education.

They have learned to listen to the universe, to see it, to
accept it as their privilege and their possession. We hope that
they will love it as their avenue to eternity and their way to
the perfection of their own immortality. We trust that they
will love with wonder the mysteries among which they move:
the sacramental vocation of water without which we cannot
have life of any kind anywhere; the momentous marriages
of the elements; the secrets of atomic existence, of all existence; the mystery and validity of thought. We want them to
continue to love, to think, to wonder, to explore their own
inheritances as children of God.

Our daughters, through their Christian education, know
that the perfection of love is service: in the normal vocation
of woman as a wife, a mother; in the state of greater perfection as a religious; but always, always as a teacher, a compassionate, merciful, normal woman finding the fulfillment of
life and of education in selfless understanding and love and
care of others.

This will not all be as sublime in the years to come as it
sounds at this moment. It can become ordinary, humdrum,
monotonous, hard. In one sense, their happiest days are
over, their care-free youth is irrevocably past, but these have
been built into a maturity limited in its goodness, its fortitude,
its incomparable womanhood only by their wills. Their
minds have been prepared.

Here I should like to quote a conversation with one of our
students some months ago. She came to my office saying: "Sister, I have a question for which I need an answer. Perhaps

you can help me." She put her question briefly and succinctly.

"I am twenty years old and have spent fourteen of these in school. By the end of college or graduate school, one-third of my life will have passed. Why am I spending so much time in school?"

Her whole state of mind was something any teacher responds to eagerly. In summary, I said to her: "But your life is never to end. You are going to live forever. Your mind, your soul is immortal. It can know and love and glorify God. In this capacity it is potentially infinite. Do you think twenty or thirty years too long to get ready to know and to love the infinity of God? Is it too long to prepare to enjoy your own immortality? Don't we need a little time to do some homework here for our life hereafter and forever?" "Sister, I thought that," she said. Her eyes filled with tears. Smiling through them, she added impatiently, "I can hardly wait."

This girl and I are going to school together and this is our reason. She is one of more than a thousand, taking the same courses in immortality, in intimations of the Beatific Vision, in love, under whatever names and numbers in our bulletin the specific classes may be listed.

We know that we are living in a secularized world, in "an apocalyptic age—a crisis of man's separation from man and of man's separation from God." Young as our daughters are, they realize that the relation between God and man implies the highest conceivable freedom—and the only one that is able to protect man from what the existentialists find the terror of existence.

In the words of Christopher Dawson, they have learned that their future and the future of the world are "found in the heart of man and the hand of God." Two thousand years ago a Roman official, "a girl at the door of an inn and a Child changed the face of the future and almost of nature." Some prayer, some spontaneous or deliberate act of spiritual acceptance or surrender on the part of our daughters may, and unquestionably does change the face of the world. This is why we are educating them.

A Christian culture and a Christian way of life are our heritage from the past and even more our hope for the future. Our daughters are the heirs to this heritage and this hope. They are the makers and the keepers of this Christian civilization. It may differ radically from our present world. Outer space may be theirs to possess and explore, but for them and through them it must be a Christian possession.

This supposes religion as well as culture. Matthew Arnold's criticism of the religion of his Victorian age still obtains. Religious people are unwilling to think. The inertia of devout, emotional complacency and physical comfort are still upon us. We are educating our daughters to think ethically, honestly, morally about civil rights, about segregation, about the sacredness of human life, about power, wealth, truth. They know, as we do, even better perhaps, that *a* world is coming to an end. They regret it perhaps less than we do.

Again quoting Christopher Dawson, "From all that we can see and from the experience of the past, it is practically certain that the period of transition will be a time of suffering." Have we been able to educate our daughters for this, for what may well be martyrdom? As Dawson says, "We know only too well how little effect the religious school has on modern secular culture and how easily the latter can assimilate and absorb the products of the religious educational system. The modern Leviathan is such a formidable monster that it can swallow the religious school system whole without suffering from indigestion.

"But this is not the case with higher education. The only part of Leviathan that is vulnerable is its brain, which is small in comparison with its vast and armored bulk. If we could develop Christian higher education to a point at which it meets the attention of the average educated man in every field of thought and life, the situation would be radically changed. . . . The trouble is that our modern secular culture is sub-literary as well as sub-religious. . . . I believe that Christians stand to gain more in the long run by accepting their minority position and looking for quality rather than quantity."

For this position of intelligence, courage, charity in a militant Christian minority, we have educated our daughters. They are moving into a world that is aiming at and striking dead moons. They are moving into a world that is denying human life to a living planet. Theirs is a generation on the highest levels of hope, the lowest depths of despair. Whether they know it or not, they are confronted with the burden, the responsibility of their greatness. Their position is not new. We read their anguish and their hope in the twenty-first chapter of the book of Isaias: "He calleth to me, Watchman, what of the night? Watchman, what of the night?" . . . "The morning cometh, and also the night: if you seek, seek: return, come."

The night may be here, may be now. This may be the hour of darkness for our era of history. It is for this and for the promised morning, the Light that is Life after the night that we are educating our daughters.

IV

The Time Is Now

MANY of us are familiar with the play by Christopher Fry, *A Sleep of Prisoners*. The story is this. Four prisoners of war, locked in a church in enemy territory, dream sequentially of Cain and Abel, David and Absalom, Abraham and Isaac, the three young men cast in the fiery furnace at the command of Nabuchodonosor. In their dreams and out of them the prisoners try to understand the world, in which they so enigmatically find themselves, and their places in it.

The play bristles with analogies. We are all prisoners in one ideology or another. An ancient Church has been violated to become a prison. We are enacting again and terribly again humanity's first murder: the fratricide of youth killed by youth. We are betrayers and betrayed. Our rulers, like David, cry out in lament at the perfidy of their disloyal favorite children. The holocaust of Abraham and Isaac sweeps our world as parents in unquestioning obedience sacrifice their sons on the altars of a freedom now long overdue. These old, Old Testament stories are our story. They have happened to us, are happening to us, through us near and far at this hour:

> Behind us lie
> The thousand and the thousand and the
>   thousand years

Vexed and terrible. And still we use
The cures which never cure.

The fourth dream has come true for many peoples in many
ages, victory over the worship of the gods of gold and power
and pride through youth's intrepid faith in God. We are
still waiting for the last dream. For us this denouement has
not yet occurred. It may be that we are already acting it. Our
world has set up gods of unbelievable power, of absolute domain. It calls this generation, which is our youth, to its defense, to its allegiance, even to its worship. It will have no
world but this and no divinity except itself.

Christianity stands against this worship of the world, this
secularism. For two thousand years the Christian school has
trained our boys and girls to repudiate and to defy it. Our
youth today is ranged before its fiery furnace. The strong, the
best of them will dare the threats of diabolism palpable in
so many places about them and will manifest in their un-
scathed Christianity the archangelic cry, "Who is like to
God?" It is to this youth, to these graduates that I wish to
speak. My first words are the magnificent declaration with
which Christopher Fry ends his play:

> Good has no fear;
> Good is itself, what ever comes.
> . . .
> Enough to subdue cities and men
> If we believe it with a long courage of truth.
> . . .
> Thank God our time is now when wrong
> Comes up to face us everywhere,
> Never to leave us till we take
> The longest stride of soul men ever took.
> Affairs are now soul size.
> The enterprise

Is exploration into God,
Where no nation's foot has ever trodden yet.

Here is your profile. Here is your future. You are as fear-
less as you are good. Your faith has the long courage and the
freedom of truth. Your education has been an education in
truth. You go out today to face wrong everywhere, to take the
longest stride your souls have ever taken. Affairs today are
all but infinite in their dimensions. Your souls outmeasure
them and can transfigure them. Your "enterprise is exploration into God." For this you have the precedents of history.
And yet you have almost no precedents for the magnitude
and the malevolence of forces ranged against this enterprise.
You meet these with and only with the omnipotence of God,
the mediation of Mary, His mother.

Fifty years ago or more we were on the threshold of the
machine age. We were told that it would be the age of the
superman, the age of science. That the superman has turned
into a Frankenstein monster is not the fault of the machine
age; it is not a defect in science. These are blind and obedi-
ent giants. It is the fault of those directing the machine, of
those applying and interpreting science. It is our fault. We
have asked the machine to give what the machine alone cannot give. We have expected of science what science alone does
not possess. We have looked to them to fulfill not only the
material but the spiritual needs of the world. We have asked
them to minister not only to the natural but to the supernatural needs of men. We have ignored the fact that these are
not their functions and are essentially outside their greatest
capacities. In our false and unfair loyalty to science and to
the machine we have refused to provide spiritual and supernatural resources for their best development. In this we have
betrayed them and betrayed ourselves. We are now in a state
of spiritual world bankruptcy, a more serious crisis than
world war. Freedom and peace depend more on a return to

supernatural values than on a victory through arms. This return can be simpler than we let ourselves believe and nearer than we permit ourselves to hope.

We describe present world conditions in superlatives. The things that are superlative in our present achievements and in our present disasters are not the all-important things. There is but one all-important and shattering tragedy in history, the Crucifixion. That is not only a mitigated, but a redeeming tragedy. There is one superlative and revolutionary sequel, the Resurrection. That is unmitigated victory. Our day and our times are keyed to these more intimately than we guess. But these transcend our world. These pervade the universe. It is the universe into which we must fit our world if we are to come to peace and freedom.

In the *Song of Bernadette,* Franz Werfel makes this caustic comment, "Your pedestrian minds are unaware of the universe." He is speaking to the townsfolk of Lourdes in 1850. Years ago Robert Louis Stevenson wrote even more cryptically, "Some people swallow the universe like a pill." Both writers address the materialists of the world, the purblind, the slogan-driven, the earth-bound, the Sancho Panzas, the opportunists. They address most of us. The ubiquitous world of Wordsworth's day has beguiled us by its magnitude and diverted us from other worlds and other heavens. The earth has been for us a big place. For many, indeed for most of its present inhabitants, it is the only place. Past and future are limited by its horizons. Our faith in it, however violently shattered, is perennial and indestructible. As children of earth we are blind to the world of the spirit. We believe more firmly in the morning paper than in the headlines of the firmament. We are unaware of the universe.

But we have opened our perilous Pandora's box with the precocious curiosity of our generation. Out of it has buzzed the radio; out of it has flown the airplane. Out of it has flashed the atom bomb. Out of it has fluttered television. They have given us a gift of tongues. They have given us wings. They have given us the flaming terror of hell, and a spurious omnipresence. They have bewitched us with petty parodies of Pentecost and the Ascension. With these new powers, we attempt the supernatural in achievement without being possessed by the supernatural in spirit or desire. The world in a decade has grown into a neighborhood. The air is our highway. The future is bounded literally by the air. This all but necessitates internationalism, a world state, and in some far, far tomorrow, world peace. But a world state will not be big enough. It must include the universe. World peace will not be peace until it is also universal. There are faith for us to retrieve and good works for us to accomplish. There is a world for us to recapture. There are precepts of peace for us to contemplate and to practice. There is freedom for us to define as well as to achieve. These two, freedom and peace, in their essence lie beyond the airways of the world. Yet there are routes to them for any man to follow.

Poets and philosophers and saints have already been profoundly aware of the universe. They have guessed rather accurately the earth's place in it. The French flyer, Antoine de Saint-Exupéry, writes in his gentle satire, *The Little Prince,* "I know a planet where there is a certain red-faced gentleman. He has never smelled a flower; he has never looked at a star; he has never loved anyone; he has never done anything in his life but add up figures; and all day he says over and over . . . 'I am busy with matters of consequence' and this makes him swell up with pride, but he is not a man—he is a mushroom."

Saint-Exupéry had made a forced landing in the Sahara, alone, a thousand miles from help, and faced with the necessity of repairing his motor by himself within the number of days his supply of drinking water would last. This comment is part of his conversation with himself, his own soul or the

Little Prince, as he calls his super-consciousness, during those strangely luminous days on the very threshold of the supernatural. The conversation continues with the Little Prince speaking:

"Where I live everything is so small. . . . The thing that is important is the thing that is not seen. All men have the stars; but they are not the same things for different people. For some who are travelers, the stars are guides; for others, they are no more than little lights in the sky; for others who are scholars, they are problems. . . . For all these, stars are silent. You will have stars that can laugh."

"This is fantasy," you may say. It is, however, the purest realism. It is the age-old music of the spheres, recaptured for us by one of the most intrepid aviators of our time with a damaged plane between himself and death on the Sahara. It is a vision of the universe so apocalyptic that it is also a vision of freedom and of peace. One hardly need add that it is poetry.

The pilot whose plane is shattered but whose faith is whole hears the laughter of the stars. The same experience lies at the heart of our great classics. It is the bitter-sweet impelling force that led Dante through the chasms of Hell, the circles of Purgatory, the heights of Paradise.

"In the middle of the journey of our life, I came to myself in a dark wood where the straight way was lost. So bitter is it that scarcely more is death," he wrote in 1300. His position parallels that of the French aviator. Out of it he was led by human wisdom to the depth of Hell; by divine wisdom, to Paradise, to the empyrean of peace, to the Beatific Vision. No one has recorded a completer vision of the universe than he. Helpless for words, he concludes his *Divine Comedy,* "O grace abounding, wherein I presumed to fix my look on the eternal light so long that I consumed my sight thereon! Within its depths I saw ingathered, bound by love in one volume, the scattered leaves of all the universe; substance and accidents and their relations, as though together fused, after such fashion that what I tell of is one simple flame. . . . To the high fantasy here power failed; but already my desire and will were rolled—even as a wheel that moveth equally—by the Love that moves the sun and the other stars." Here is not only a world at peace, but a universe at peace. Of it Dante says simply, "His will is our peace." A more perfect definition of peace has not been written.

On a less exalted plane, Chaucer crystallizes this conviction and echoes this experience in the conclusion of his *Troilus and Criseyde*. He was writing of the Trojan war, remote from his own day by some thousands of years. Troilus, the greatest Trojan except Hector, had been killed by Achilles. His death had been precipitated by the crassest of treacheries. It had been exalted by a profound and idealized love. Chaucer looked at his death in battle not as a finality in time, but under the aspect of eternity. The poet, who was aware of the universe and knew the melody of the stars, writes of the hero's death:

> And when that he was slayn in this manere,
> His lighte goost ful blisfully is went
> Up to the holughnesse of the eighthe spere,
> In convers letyng everich element;
> And ther he saugh, with ful avysement,
> The erratik sterres, herkenyng armoyne
> With sownes ful of hevenyssh melodie.
>
> And down from thennes faste he gan avyse.
> This wrecched world, and held al vanite
> This litel spot of erthe, that with the se
> Emmbraced is, and fully gan despise
> In respect of the pleyn felicite
> That is in hevene above; . . .

And in hymself he lough right at the wo
Of hem that wepten for his deth so faste.

The siege of Troy is history's great classic metaphor for
world war. Not Paris, nor Hector, nor Menelaus but Troilus
is the protagonist. In the apocalypse of death, against one
moment of the felicity of heaven, he sees this little spot of
earth. Intuitively, he knows its wretchedness and vanity. He
laughs in his achieved freedom and peace. This laughter is
the laughter of the stars. He sees the universe forever. These
really are what most of the world is fighting for, the supernatural qualities of peace and freedom. They come only
through the avenues of the supernatural.

While Chaucer was writing this an amazing thing was
taking place in Norwich, a hundred miles north of his London
home. A woman, known to the world as Dame Julian, was
living as a recluse in a hermitage beside the Church of Saint
Julian in Norwich. The church still stands in the busy English
town, better known to us for its great cathedral, the burial
place of Edith Cavell. The anchorhold of the great mystic,
Dame Julian, is reverently marked and the authenticity of
her experience is unquestioned by critics today. Indeed, in
his volume, *Four Quartets,* T. S. Eliot quotes directly from
the thirty-second chapter of her autobiography.

This obscure woman, in her thirtieth year, experienced in
the course of two days sixteen revelations of the passion and
death of Christ. The record of them, entitled *Sixteen Revelations of Divine Love,* is one of the great spiritual classics
of the world. It contains such statements as this:

"I saw God in a point," which is a simplification of Dante's
"one simple flame." It contains this equally concise and
amazing vision of the universe:

"And in this Christ shewed a little thing, the quantitie of
a hasel-nutt, lying in the palme of my hand, as me seemed;

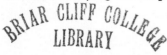

and it was as round as a ball. I looked thereon with the eie of my understanding, and thought, 'What may this be?' and it was answered generallie thus:

" 'It is all that is made.' "

These fourteenth century airviews of the earth challenge our thought and dwarf our conquest of the skies. The radio has put its girdle around the earth in less than forty minutes and has outdistanced Puck. The airplane has dropped on Prospero's island from the blue. The atomic, electronic, nuclear powers are ours in the terrifying ambiguity of slaves and masters. But they have not caught the harmony of the erratic stars and their "hevenyssh melodie," nor beheld all created being in a nutshell. Nor have they risen with Dante to the ninth circle of paradise, nor dreamed the ecstasy of its empyrean. Their exploitation of the air is earthbound still. They embrace every known law of the skies except this ultimate law, "His will is our peace." And so although physically they win the air, they lose this peace.

Edwin Arlington Robinson was, at his death in 1935, a proud figure in American letters, three times a Pulitzer prize winner for poetry. Of our generation, he says, "The world is not a prison house but a kind of spiritual kindergarten where millions of infants are trying to spell God with the wrong blocks." The world is still a kindergarten. We have lost the blocks that spell God. We have thrown aside the blocks that spell the universe. We are looking for the blocks that spell peace, for the blocks that spell freedom: freedom of speech, freedom of religion, freedom from want, and freedom from fear. But no one has tried to free us from our fear of belief in God. No one has tried to free us from our want of faith in Christ. No one has thought of the Lord's prayer as a refuge from fear, of the Apostles' Creed as food against spiritual starvation.

Nicholas Murray Butler said in an address, "What Does

Freedom Mean?" "The essentials of the Christian religion are to be found in the three most important documents which history records: the Ten Commandments, the Lord's Prayer, and the Apostles' Creed. . . . Religious freedom will not have been fully achieved until these fundamental facts and principles are realized and acted upon." Our present freedom is the freedom of blackouts, not the freedom of the stars, not the freedom of the universe. It is the freedom of cities plunged in air shelters, not the ultimate freedom of "the man who is open to God and plunged in Him."

Nevertheless, the world of the air is a promised land. The tragedy of the machine age, of the age of science is not the failure of faith but the failure of faith in the supernatural. Faith in much of the Christian world is dead. It died, as Christianity always dies, of crucifixion. The Pharisees of our day, the moneychangers, the barterers in flesh and blood are stricken by darkness over the face of the world and by ghosts returning from uneasy graves. Centurions are striking their breasts; rulers are washing their hands; and traitors are hanging themselves with halters. Their heaped up monies of betrayal have bought continents for potters' fields.

But history teaches us the fact of the Resurrection of Christ. The Apostles' Creed teaches us the fact of the resurrection of the body. This is one of the most neglected of all the articles of that creed. Yet it is for us the most exciting and personal. It should fascinate us beyond all the thrills of radio and aviation. For it is an experience as inevitable as death that will come to everyone. It is an experience about which we never think, the resurrection of the body; that my body will be restored to me after death with qualities of immortality: with lucidity, agility, impassibility. This means that with my risen body, I shall be able to go from place to place with the immediacy of thought; that I shall experience no physical imperfection, sickness, or death; that I can pass through a mountain range as easily as through a sunbeam; that I myself shall provide the necessary light for any possible darkness in my environment. It means that I am and possess the super-airways, the super-air systems not only of the world but of the universe. It is not unsignificant that our most influential inventions in an age of materialism have been bent on recapturing through matter and force the attributes of our glorified bodies. They stand as eloquent intimations of the resurrection of the body. It is not unsignificant that more than one boy under military training today has described our air force as a poor parody of the Ascension. This world of the air which we now possess can lead us into a promised land. It can reveal the world of brotherhood, a Christian country, an earthly paradise.

Antoine de Saint-Exupéry asks us to listen to the laughter of the stars. Dante lifts us beyond them to the Beatific Vision. Chaucer looks down with celestial laughter on this little spot of earth. Dame Julian sees it saved by the love of God. They were all spokesmen for times as troubled and as cataclysmic as our own. They are great challenges to our conquest of the air and our shaping of an air-bound peace. They reveal to us a universe without which we can never come to peace. They rest upon the greatest of all gospels of peace, that preached from the air over the hills of Bethlehem on the night that Christ was born.

It has been said that our mechanical development has outstripped our intellectual and sociological preparation. We are not ready to administer a world state made possible by air navigation. What of Christianity? What of the Beatitudes? What of the mystical body of Christ? What in all our atom-smashing conquest outstrips these? Where apart from them is a promise of peace tenable to men?

Let us return to our own day, to our own continent. Paul Claudel was an astute statesman. He was an experienced mystic. He was a profound dramatic poet. His books are a composite of the three. In the language of enigma they reveal deep and often terrifying truth. But in their truth is freedom of spirit, the only security that is not a trap and a betrayal.

In conclusion, I should like to speak of one of the least known of the plays of Claudel. It has a pertinence to us as Americans. It has prophetic value to us as teachers and students. It is the *Book of Christopher Columbus*. The name of the book is its theme. Christopher Columbus was literally the Christ-bearer, the dove. He was a mariner sailing under these divine and double orders. In a sense his discovery of America created a vast and double continent and a vaster ocean beyond. It extended the known universe for the Christian world. More momentous than that, it brought Christ to this continent. It revealed God and the Gospel of Christ to the souls inhabiting these strange lands. The implications of these familiar facts are eternally important.

But for Christopher Columbus the greatest and most devastating adventure was his continuing discovery of the will of God. Beset by mutiny, he dropped his compass, a foolish toy, into the sea. The will of God was the magnetic pole by which he charted his course, the country to which he sailed. The will of God was his wedded love and endless life. Chains and prison were the world's thankless prelude to the paradise of this idea, the beatific vision of this discovery.

The *Book of Christopher Columbus* is the story of every student. Tomorrow and tomorrow and tomorrow lie before you and your undiscovered worlds. You are Christ-bearers to them. You are co-creators of worlds of the mind, bringing tidings of truth into a future yet unguessed by you, and the gospel of faith and hope and love. Does it seem a vague and profitless adventure? Please believe me when I say that it is a career as well as a vocation. It can be realized in ways as diverse as you yourselves are.

You are bearers of peace and the dove. You take with you

unguessed gifts of the Spirit, gifts and graces which, since the days of the first Pentecost, have lifted men up and restored them to their normal level of the children of God.

Most of you are discoverers, in quest of your native land, which is the will of God. Every other destination that you may have in mind at this moment or ever is dependent on this. The magnetic north that guides you, the undiscovered country that awaits you must be this infinite will.

We will not promise you happiness. We will not wish you security. For we remember that "security is mortal's chiefest enemy." And we know that you can be secure only when you can stand everything that can happen to you. If your school has prepared you for this, it has been a good school. We promise you discovery, the discovery of yourselves, the discovery of the universe and your place in it.

With these unguessed, untried potencies you begin your lifetime enterprise of exploration into God. Affairs are now and always, for you, soul-size.

V

The Poetics of the College Woman

POETRY, perhaps the oldest of the fine arts, is the one now somewhat fallen into disuse. To what end some of us know experimentally. No one among us is ever completely untouched by having poetry in the intellectual air we breathe, the intellectual fare on which our minds are fed.

This being so, let us consider the poetics of college education, the making of the college woman. This takes us back into the origin of the word "poetics." It is a derivative from the Greek, meaning "to make" or "the art of making." The person who does this, who exercises this art, is the poet, the maker. But first he must see the possibilities within persons, places, things for such making, such creation. First, he must be a seer. He must have vision, insight. This, in certain magnitudes, constitutes inspiration.

The seer, if he is a true seer, cannot stop here. He must give form to what he sees; he must express his vision; he must make a worthy image of it. He must become a maker.

If the thing that he sees is of overwhelming beauty he tries to match this beauty with his expression of it. He not only makes it palpably, he sings it. All in all, he is a seer, a maker, a singer.

This is the experience of every poet. This is his craft and

his art. This, in the limited use of the word, is what we mean by poetics.

But there can be quite properly a poetics of every art: the seeing, the making, the singing of music, of the graphic arts, of fiction, of the sciences surely. There is a poetics of education, the creative process of making, through the vision of truth, of charity, the emotional intensities of goodness and beauty, out of a responsive girl a responsible woman.

The entire process is one of sublimation or inspired making, communication on so high a level of love and beauty that the telling or saying of it becomes a singing, becomes a song. The end of the poetics of the college girl should be a poem, the college woman.

Please do not mistake this as a mere play with words. It is in the deepest sense a diagnosis of what is happening to each one of you. You will never be the subject or the object of a diviner comedy than this in which you are now engaged, the poetics of your own education, the making of your own womanhood.

You have often been told that you are now in the golden years of your lives. You will never be more beautiful, never more intelligent. You can anticipate, to fulfill your present promise, the magnitudes of experience, the serenities of wisdom, the charms of charity. But these are yet to come and can be acquired only in terms of time plus.

To the poetics of the woman you are to be, through the arts of your college, you have brought the basic materials of physical and academic preparation. Yours are the indispensable sound minds in sound bodies. Yours, too, is the environment described by Newman as ideal for the intellectual life: "a certain remoteness from the confusion of the market place and the crowd, a serenity of atmosphere, a freedom of spirit, the clear and open skies of thought, the wonder and tranquility of order, peace." This may not appear to you as a description of your *status quo*. But if it is not, you will never know it—never more than now, surely.

You are in this felicitous environment because those who care for you are seers; your parents, your teachers have seen in you the promise of sturdy, courageous, intelligent womanhood. Your own concern with your lives as gifts and promises has supported these hopes. The insight, the vision of the seer, often amounting to inspiration, preface the great work of poetics.

We come now to the process of making proper, which is for you the process of learning. This involves, as we have said to you before, the most intimate and mysterious of all human relationships. Shakespeare has called it "the marriage of true minds" and so it is; the attitudes of mutual attraction, the generosities of giving and receiving, the humilities of forming and being formed, the immortal bonds of teacher and student. All of these exist between you and each of your teachers. Every class leaves you in some way changed. Every teacher has a part in your making, the poetics of your educated womanhood.

These intellectual unions are entered into for their own sakes, as ends in themselves. Your minds, in their proper functioning, are yourselves and need no better reason for their development than do you for your existence.

An even better reason, however, does exist. We enter into this enterprise of the poetics, this making of you as educated women for God's sake. We are made to His image, to begin with. Every right determination of our minds, our intellects, perfects that resemblance. We are even now His daughters. The perfection of education can realize in us the epic, the lyric, the canticle of being. It has not yet appeared what we shall be.

Obviously, in and through and over all this education, this matter of making and saying and singing, God is the prime poet. Only the teachers who instruct in His presence know the supernatural joy of their work. Only those who share their knowledge, their students, their academic odysseys with Mary and the great hosts of angels and saints, experience the skyscraping excitements of such traffic between mortality and immortality, between space and the infinities.

The poetics of your education becomes the work of many masters. We must not overlook some of the most potent, your classmates, your friends. Every one of you has some part in the making of every other student. This is a fact, a privilege, a responsibility. Let me ask you to assume these mutual responsibilities, act upon them. You are all artisans in the poetics of educated womanhood, the making of good women. The perfected poetics will be a song, will be poetry. You are in this capacity poets. More than that, you are immortal poets.

Let me submit three cases in point. About ten years ago Jack and Mary Grace of two good neighbor contemporary colleges were married, much against the wishes of Mary Grace's mother. Her constant reproach was, "Now what will your $10,000 education do for you?"

Some years later, Mary Grace left her two little girls and baby boy playing in the yard with a most dependable nurse. The nurse went into the house on an errand. In that irretrievable moment, the baby fell into the shallow pool and smothered. A half hour later Mary Grace came home to find her little son dead. Out of her frantic grief and incredulity, one thought emerged, "Whatever is, is adorable." This sublimated acceptance of the will of God, in whatever guise, the poetics of her education had given her this, her answer to her mother: "This is what my $10,000 education has done for me."

Some years earlier one of our most brilliant and sophisticated graduates chose to marry, from among many suitors, a man from Mexico. Six months ago their tenth baby was born, a little girl named Madeleva. In her Christmas note to me Nona Mae wrote, "Perhaps you have heard that our baby, who was supposed to emulate her namesake, is probably mentally retarded and will never be older than age five. She is a darling and in a hurry, hurry, competitive world, it is quite wonderful to have a child who has already achieved heaven by *being* only." This, I submit, is quite beyond poetry.

The same Christmas mail brought a letter from Shirley Kalina, now a novice in the Convent of the Good Shepherd. In describing the order of her days, she says, "We study Christian Doctrine and the work of our Order, but mostly we study Love."

Have I overstated the poetics of education, the making of the educated woman? These are realities that have come into being here in your world and your generation.

Christopher Fry, in his play, *The Dark is Light Enough,* says of the heroine, a woman of supernatural charity,

Lives make and unmake themselves in her neighborhood
As nowhere else . . .
She has a touching way
Of backing a man up against eternity
Until he hardly has the nerve to remain mortal.

This can be true of persons. It can be true of places. At your college, it is true of both.

VI

Cassandra Speaks on Poetry

HAVE you ever asked the question, "What per cent of college students think?" One hundred per cent is not the answer, nor even 50 per cent. For graduate students, the correct answer is probably lower than that.

Both our methods of education and our prevailing types of examinations train our students to remember and to imitate rather than to think. The original and creative thinker in a class can be a difficult student. The potential poet is an original and a creative thinker.

One of the most provocative sentences in our language is "Just think!" One of our lamest alibis is "I didn't think." Our proper prerogative of thinking has given place in our speech, if not in practice, to feeling. We report usually on what we feel, how we feel, or what our feeling is on a matter rather than what our thinking is. The two are different. The poet is a specialist in both.

Jacques Maritain lifts these activities to their perfect level. He says that "Man is called to supernatural contemplation." Contemplation is, by definition, "intent study or consideration." Supernatural contemplation is concerned with the metaphysical, the divine, with Deity itself. The word denotes all this. Etymologically, it means the act of being in a temple.

Consideration means the act of being among the stars. We could hardly be more contemporary. And this is our vocation as persons.

Suppose we reject this vocation. Suppose we repudiate this heritage. Again, Maritain says, "To turn away from wisdom and contemplation and to aim lower than God is in a Christian civilization the first cause of all disorder." This we have been doing, wittingly or unwittingly, for generations. Today we find ourselves in a state of international disorder, in a condition of world revolution. Our turning away from wisdom may very well be the first cause of this *status quo*. The poet can be what George Barker calls our "providential" defender. The poet can lead us back to the wisdom that is truth and the truths that are wisdom. Only he can report anything like the truth in present society.

Who or what is a poet? What are his wares, what is poetry? Aristotle calls the poet a seer, a maker, a singer. Maritain defines poetry as "the divination of the spiritual in the things of sense." Again we find ourselves in the area of the temple and among the stars. In pagan times, divination was a sharing of the secrets of the gods. In a Christian world, it is being inspired or breathed into by the Holy Spirit. But who wants to share the secrets of the gods? Who wants to be breathed into by the Holy Spirit? Who wants to be a seer, a singer? Who wants to be a poet?

Someone raised the question recently, "Are poets necessary?" This constructive question from a doctor at the Lahey Clinic takes away some of the bitter taste from our literary mouths. He asked, "Do you think that enough poetry is being taught in our schools today? My children do not even know how to read poetry. We used to get so much joy out of it."

We have penetrated the secrets of the atom. We have invented and researched ourselves into possible annihilation. Our missile piles are a terror rather than a triumph. Electronics has stunned us into automation. The wise man in

Solomon's day lamented, "when vision fails the nation perishes." What future might he have predicted for the nation where thinking fails? George Barker protests bitterly against "the spiritual irresponsibility of a world that pays millions of dollars for a bomb and forty shillings for a poem."

A great world and a great work are open to us as students and teachers, the worlds and work of contemplation and creative thought, of insight, of the divination of the spiritual in the world of our five senses. The translation of our discoveries into the language of beauty should follow. We should see visions. We should dream dreams. We should write poems. All of us can be seers. Most of us can be makers. Some of us can be singers.

Are these sufficiently impelling reasons for reading and writing poetry? Perhaps not, but there are others, fascinating ones. As you remember from Molière's *Le Bourgeois Gentilhomme*, everything that is not prose in verbal communication is poetry. It is one of the two great modes of communication. We can express ourselves, in words, in no other ways. The choices are limited. We should be pleased to use both, poetry and prose. Some of us do. More of us ought to.

Poetry is an art. The poet is an artist, a creator of beauty, the maker of a home of words, strong and richly adequate for the thought they domesticate. The philosopher is the discoverer, the definer of truth. The poet is the architect of the house of words in which truth may dwell.

What grace is to the moral life poetry is to art, supernaturalizing and transfiguring the simplest, the common things. It ministers spiritual nourishment to our emotional needs. The Psalms, our favorite lyric poems, are the poems we turn to in our great joys, our profound sorrows.

Let us see our assignment in its right demands and dimensions. Poetry is hard work, disciplined work, requiring the exact word for the exact thought in the exact and proper position. It can provide a relative answer for the question with which we began this discussion, "What per cent of college students think?" Every student who reads or tries to write poetry thinks. "Poetry," Maritain tells us, "is the heaven of the working reason." This is both a definition and a reward. Heaven is a place of complete happiness. The working reason should find divine content in the poet's world. Where else does one meet with such inducements?

Our talk on poetry has employed a discursive method. We have meant to offer a plea for the reclamation of a heritage, a promised land, an all-but-lost-Eden for our youth today. Many of them stand at the gates. They want to think, to contemplate. They want to enter the temple of supernatural truth, to move among the stars of divine wisdom. Some of them want to sing of this experience. Some want to be poets.

We have in our great scientific achievements modern parodies for our nursery rhymes: our satellites jumping over the moon, our Jacks and their bean stalks plundering the planets. Presently, we may put into orbit a young woman sailing fifty times as high as the moon. Perhaps we can conclude with another analogy from our childhood. Perhaps poetry is our Sleeping Beauty. Who will break through the wilderness of spurious feeling and writing to her world of beauty and truth? Who will wake her? Who will kiss her back to life?

VII

Educating Our Daughters as Women

A COLLEGE board of trustees is an excellent tribunal before which to test our theories and practices in the education of our daughters. Individually, these trustees have academic interests as wide and as varied as their professions, their industries, their immediate occupations. Within their own localities, they may be working on a hospital project, a new elementary school or a high school. They may be concerned with programs in nursing, in education. We can lead them down all the paths and bypaths of academic specialization with varying responses of interest or inquiry. For the most part they have moved away from the worlds of educational theory to the stern realities of practice. One question is common to all of them. This they ask: "Does anyone think of educating a woman as a woman?"

The question pulls us up sharply. Basically we face a double problem in education. Should the college educate a woman as a woman? If so, how? These are two questions that suggest a third equally important one: Do all types of college educate our daughters equally well in their proper vocation of being women?

Running the gantlet of semantics, we may say that we always educate a woman as a woman. The quantity and quality of her womanhood depend very much, first upon herself; then upon the school that she attends, the school that is her Alma Mater. She will probably resemble her intellectual mother. Our trustees may have in mind a quintessence of womanliness as a quality to be preserved, if not indeed to be developed in the education of our daughters. We believe in the quintessence of womanliness as the very flower and fruit of the education of women.

These daughters of ours have had two choices in the kind of college training they wished: coeducation or education in the private college for women. If they chose the latter, they elected to be educated as women with an existential major and minor in womanhood. Their academic choices became effective in this environment, in this their essential existence. Their entire life, their worlds, their unguessed futures have already received certain determinations, certain directions by this choice.

They may go to coeducational schools. Why not? Coeducational universities and colleges educate young women in exactly the same way as they educate men. In fact all of our coeducational schools on the college level, until within the past decade perhaps, began as schools for men. Women were admitted first cautiously and by exception. Once matriculated, they proved, by and large, their ability to be educated in the same way as men or in curricula set up for men. Gradually departments in home economics and nursing were provided specifically for women. Today they constitute a large percentage of the enrollment in coeducational schools. Tens of thousands of our American girls are in college with hundreds of thousands of our American boys, and love it. They emerge as educated women, but not quite the same type of women they might have been if they had been educated as women.

These are merely statements of fact. They are neither a measure of the value of coeducation to our daughters, or of our daughters to coeducation. The value of girls on the co-educational campus is pervasive, subtle. It has something to do with ties, with grooming in general, with the gentle arts of courtesy. Recently a newspaper published the picture of a student carrying his girl friend's books. This was front-page news. Upon a time one of our best American universities reported the registration of two pretty young women in the graduate school as effecting a palpable return to the fine arts and courtesies of living among these high-grade men students.

Girls do not go to coeducational schools for these reasons, but they do affect coeducation in these ways. Reciprocally, their coeducational colleges affect them. A girl educated with, and as boys are educated, will be a different woman from the girl educated as girls are and with them.

This does not imply that they are, or should be educated exclusively by women. The better the college for women, the healthier ballast of scholarly men it will invite to its faculty. The mind of a growing girl realizes its capacities more perfectly under the tutelage of both scholarly men and scholarly women. This is true for boys as well. Men are quick and proud to recognize this.

But as boys, they do not clamor to go to colleges for women; they do not stampede our private schools and insist on being educated as girls are educated. We women have reversed the story of the Sabine women; we have put ourselves in a somewhat unintellectual position in our very endeavor to prove our intellectual equality with men.

For more than a century and a quarter our girls have had excellent colleges for women from which to choose. They select this type of school because they want this experience of the intellectual life as and with young women. Most of them do not change their minds on this score during their four undergraduate years.

Just how might a college educate young women as women?

It might recognize the great fields of knowledge, the sciences, the liberal arts, the fine arts. Since theology is the queen of the sciences it might make it the core, the central and integrating subject in the curriculum. The student's entire experience can become significant in terms of its relation to God. The student herself will grow in the knowledge of her own supernatural stature in consequence, and of the supernatural world itself in which we all live and move. Her womanhood will be measured by, and uplifted to the womanhood of Mary. This in itself educates her as a woman.

Around the science of theology, the profane sciences range themselves in orders and potencies which atomic energies and electronics merely shadow. Women can move among these as freely as men, with the authentic freedom of truth. Such fields as cancer research and care of premature babies are being successfully investigated by teachers and students in colleges for women. They are living in their Father's house, working with His tools, playing at times perhaps with the fascinating toys He has provided for them. This is far from fancy. The greatest scientists know it to be a divine fact.

The liberal arts are most liberal, most liberating when they rest on complete rather than on partial truth. Here the Catholic college was the authentic exponent for the first sixteen centuries of Christian arts and sciences. One may say the same of the fine arts. Also, girls study, learn, and respond to teaching differently from the way boys do, and differently in classes with boys from the way they do in groups of girls only. Whatever the reasons for the delicate psychology governing these facts, they are facts. Girls achieve a type of womanhood when educated with girls which differs from the results of coeducation. We believe that this difference is a more refined, a more perfect womanhood, the quintessential womanliness.

Perfection is not achieved without costs. The women's colleges in the United States are monuments to the enterprise, the sacrifice, the fortitude of women. They are the most expensive to maintain, the last to benefit by philanthropy. Present educational crises are being met by colossal gifts from corporations, foundations, individuals.

At a recent meeting of the American Council on Education, the question was asked, "Where in the order of these gifts do colleges for women stand?" This is the answer which was given, not without embarrassment, "Gifts for education go first, to schools with big names; second, to big schools; third, to coeducational schools; fourth, to women's colleges." Considering that half the parents of the world, all of the mothers, the wives, the daughters, and the sisters are women, this does not reflect gloriously to the generosity, the chivalry, the gratitude, or even the justice of the manhood of our country.

We come back to the question with which we began: "Are we educating our daughters as women?" We have put before our hypothetical tribunal of college trustees our two general answers. Coeducation does not educate our daughters essentially as women. The woman's private college does. Its survival is precarious, since it is the last and the least supported of all the colleges in our educational structure. We can continue to educate our daughters as women only with adequate help. Our men who have been educated as men know the answer. The education of our daughters as women depends upon them.

VIII

That Not Impossible She

THREE hundred years ago the English poet, Richard Crashaw, wrote a poem, entitled *Wishes to His Supposed Mistress:*

> Whoe'er she be,
> That not impossible she,
> That shall command my heart and me.

It is a dexterously written, delicately veiled poem to the Blessed Virgin. Three hundred years ago poems in praise of Our Lady were not the most popular form of English literature. They were best veiled for safety's sake.

Without doing overmuch violence to Crashaw's lovely lines we might appropriate them to you. We might regard each one of you as "that not impossible she." We might speak to you.

Four years ago you came to college. Why did you come? Can you remember, or do you know? Reasons have changed so in that short lifetime that some have lost their validity, others their importance. At this moment the first home game, the first date, the first formal seem rather remote and young among the essentials of your education. Still, they had their places. The first pink slips (if any) have lost their menace and the first semester examinations their terror. Vacation hegiras and tumultuous returns total to a confusion of gay memories. The ghosts of comprehensives and final examinations now rest in quiet graves. What did you come to college for? Nothing in the form of all your accumulated furniture, wardrobe, souvenirs that will travel home with you betrays the nature of your quest or its fulfillment.

This I count among the memorable experiences of many years of college teaching and administration. A freshman came into my office with her class cards. She put them down on my desk for inspection. "I am taking these subjects," she said, "to develop my mind." Her simple, succinct statement may be your answer. You came to college, each one of you, to develop your mind, to change your mind many times, many ways, and for many reasons. All of them should have been good. The results should be a better mind than you brought to college and a better young woman than the girl you were four years ago.

Without digressing, let us get out two of the great books of your world, your high school senior and your college senior yearbooks. Turn to your pictures in both; the same girl, but you are different. Even photography proves it. Supposing that we could replace these pictures with photographs of your mind. Your parents, you and, I think, even your teachers would be pleased with what has happened to your mind.

You came to college with the ideas of a girl. You leave college with the ideas of a young woman. You came to college with the ideals of a girl. You leave college with the ideals of a thoughtful woman. You came to college with a teachable mind, a mind open to truth, open to God, a will responsive to His will. You leave college with a mind instructed in truth, possessed by God, a will strengthened by four years of close companionship with Him, of obedience to His will. Paraphrasing the Oriental proverb, you brought riches to India; you are taking riches from India. You came to a Catholic college most of all because of your personal friendship for God, for Mary His mother. This has intensified through your companionship with Jesus in your college chapels, through His letters to you in the Sacred Scriptures, through your lived life in His mystical body, the Church.

In all of this, speaking with the tongues of men and of angels, we may not be understood in the market place, the world to which the highways from college will carry you. Can you take your college with you? Can you speak this language intelligently, fearlessly to it? The polysyllables that you have heard oftenest with their dire implications these past four years are materialism, secularism, Communism, minorities, atom bomb, annihilation. Their reality in current thinking comes true in such statements as these, quoted from recent symposiums on *Religion and the Intellectuals,* and *Freedom and Reason:*

". . . there is no realm outside nature, and everything must be found within this world.

". . . the fact is that the intellectual substructure of super- naturalist religions, including Christianity, has now been washed away. . . .

"The concept of the supernatural is a disease of reli- gion . . . Christian supernaturalism is equally a disease of language. . . .

"By nature man is a creature who can make his own history. But he did not make the world in which that history is open to him. Because he did not make the world is not a valid ground for the belief that any other species did—natural or supernatural. . . . Man in fact relies on his own natural and human resources even when he claims to rely on other re- sources."

These are the doctrines of the world on whose threshold you stand. Can you take your college and your college educa- tion with you into it? You go out as a member of a minority on three counts: a Catholic, a graduate of a private school, a

Catholic college. Your advent may be more opportune than that of the tens of thousands of graduates now emerging from our great universities. You are an eternity ahead of this group of contemporary intellectuals presented in *Time* magazine:

"Twenty-five years ago, traditional Christianity seemed to many an American intellectual to be rolling up the scroll. The Good Life was a matter of well-planned getting and spending, and all the answers were to be found written down, from Hegel to Freud to Keynes. Professor John Dewey and his fellow philosophers were preaching a heady trial and error pragmatism. The up-to-date intellectual was so uninterested in Christianity that he rarely found it worth while even to be anti-religious.

"Today in the U.S. the Christian faith is back in the center of things, with an intellectual respectability that has not been accorded it in generations. . . . Bestseller lists are crowded month after month with books with religious themes. The seminaries are crowded with the kind of young men the secular world competes for. . . . Even among the skeptical, the Western world considers the question: Is it possible that Christianity is really true after all?"

Waiving the condescension, the invincibly ignorant sacrilege of the statements, you and your college have infallible answers. As Charles Lindbergh said recently: "The chaos of our modern world is staggering . . . but when we . . . release in it the catalyst of faith, the future clarifies."

Take your college and its teaching with you to your Western world with its bewildered, battered, and beaten query, "Is it possible that Christianity is really true, after all?" Answer it with your faith, your hope. Best of all, answer it with love. You have both the responsibility of a faithful love of truth and a loving concern for those who are seeking it. Traditional Christian Protestantism is returning to the environs of its father's house. For twenty-five years its prodigal sons have fed on the husks of Hegel and Freud, have lived behavioristically with Dewey and Keynes. The raiment of truth and the feast of Christian charity should welcome them home. You can be hostesses in your Father's house.

This world into which you go has troubles worse than dreams and complexes, and urges. It must, as Dr. Henry Pitney Van Dusen, director of the Union Theological Seminary, says, face the four last things: death, judgment, hell, heaven. American Protestants, he says, "must come to grips with a term almost as unfamiliar to their ears as was the term 'ecumenical' twenty or even ten years ago—the term 'eschatological.' " Not only must they accustom their ears to the sound of the word; they must give their minds and hearts to the attempt to comprehend it and why it holds so decisive, so pivotal a place in the hope of fellow Christians in many lands and of many traditions.

"But above all, they should re-examine critically the nature and ground of their own hope as Christians, in order that they may give a clear, convinced and convincing account of the faith that is in them."

You can take not only your four-year college but your very childhood with you to this perplexed world that is trying to spell God with the wrong blocks. As children you lived with and talked about this big polysyllable, eschatology, which means death, judgment, hell, heaven. The first sentence of the "Our Father" takes us to heaven. The Apostles' Creed prepares us for judgment. It implies hell and promises us heaven. The "Hail Mary" cares for the very hour of our death. These tremendous realities you have known since you were six years old. Can you take them to your twentieth century world? Will you? You must do it with simplicity and love. Perhaps you can lead it past the terrifying shadows of eschatology to the splendors of its beatitude.

Twenty centuries ago, a girl not too unlike you, lived with

her Son and her husband in an obscure town in Galilee. The whole world honors her today. In her lifetime she belonged to a minority smaller than yours. Let us not underestimate the strength and the rightness of minorities. Again I quote Charles Lindbergh: "We must remember that it was not the outer grandeur of the Roman but the inner simplicity of the Christian that lived on through the ages." This young girl of Galilee, this Mary of Nazareth, is the Mother of Christians. You can take her to the world estranged from her. It has no greater need. You are the daughters of her college. You go out to receive her heritage. This, in the words of Gilbert Chesterton, is what she offers you as legacy:

> But you and all the kind of Christ
>   Are ignorant and brave,
> And you have wars you hardly win
>   And souls you hardly save.
>
> I tell you naught for your comfort,
>   Yea, naught for your desire,
> Save that the sky grows darker yet
>   And the sea rises higher.

Again we ask, "Why did you come to college?" Can you take it with you? We have said only the first word of your reply. The entire answer will not be an easy one. The world may fear to be destroyed mortally with atomic forces. You can help to save it immortally with sanctifying grace. Your world may be defying space and gravity to reach the sterility of a dead moon. You can teach it to outdistance space ships en route to heaven and the Beatific Vision.

And even while the sky grows darker and the sea rises higher we see above the chaos of our days something of what a girl saw a hundred years ago at Lourdes, what three peasant children looked on within the lifetime of your parents:

We see a queen most womanly—
But she is a queen of men.

Over the iron forest
We see our Lady stand,
Her eyes are sad withouten art,
And seven swords are in her heart
But one is in her hand.

We began by talking of education, Mary, and you. They are the dearest trinity of your college life. You can take them with you. You can be their central force and purpose, the Christian woman. In his own war-worn France Charles Péguy exclaimed explosively, "What we need, God, what we finally need is a woman who would also be a saint."

Mary, you are wise, you are brave, you are our world's first love, you are a woman. Gird every college graduate with the armor of your seven swords. Gird her to become that militant, that merciful, that not impossible she, a woman who is also a saint.

IX

What Are Mothers Like?

WE ARE faced with no dearth of subjects in fields of current education. We might talk of college enrollments. We might speak of housing facilities, necessary to billet this great academic army. We might consider the faculties, the college teachers required to train and discipline these troops, our greatest national and international defense. We might ask the billion-dollar question, "Who is going to finance all of this? What legion of angels will pick up the tab?" The Federal Government, corporations, foundations, philanthropy are pooling their resources to teach our children, our youth their A B C's. They are reaching out to the whole world, so deeply do we believe in you, in youth. No cause, except national defense, is undertaken with such generosity, with such unquestioning love.

There are the great problems of human relations, academic freedom, national and international, desegregation in fact and in practice as well as in law.

Sound public relations are becoming more and more important to the college as are vocational preparation, professional leadership, international education. On our campuses the place of the fine arts in the college curriculum is assuming eminence, promising rich possibilities and permanent values in life.

All these are focused on our futures. There seems to be no such time as today. If and when today comes we recognize it as the tomorrow we had spent so much time preparing for.

We might talk of this tenuous today, this present, this here and now, and its problems. These include student-faculty relationships and their basic policies, student participation in curriculum building, college development programs, student leadership and government, college publications.

We might enter upon that perennial subject, the school itself, and the spirit of the school, upon our most and our least intelligent gripes, their causes and effects. Then, there are the brand new subjects that have not yet had cigarette ashes spilled on them; the girls (and they are splendidly distinguished) who have the courage to be themselves; what is right with the school; what the school does with your ten-dollar lecture fees? You recognize this all as a part of the cumulative experience that we know as "going to college."

Also, there is your future, the vague horizons of which become clearer, more demanding as your four years near their end. They embrace, not next summer, or next year; they mark out your places in the world, an international world, for the next fifty years. They carry you into the millennium, the year 2000 and onward. They carry you into eternity. To share these enigmatic years, to venture into this unprecedented future, you are being wooed by many suitors. Science wants you. Industry loves you. Education exalts you. Nursing hallows you. Social service implores you. Your future lies in all these worlds; in some of them rather more than but not to the exclusion of the others.

There is a future toward which you are all moving, for which each one of you has been specifically made and for which your years at college are intentionally preparing you. I should like to tell you of this through the story of *Marcelino,* a Spanish legend recaptured by Sanchez-Silva and translated by Angela Britton.

Marcelino was a foundling, left on the steps of a Franciscan monastery outside a little town in Spain more than 100 years ago. Spanish Franciscans have not at any time been perfect baby sitters. But they loved little Marcelino and took him into their grown-up world as a friar decidedly minor. For all their manly company, the little boy missed playmates, companions of his own age. Animals were his playthings: the philosophical old goat, the captive toad, the quick darting lizard, grasshoppers, beetles, and Mutchy, the friary cat.

The boy often wondered about himself, about his father, mother, brothers, and sisters which he knew other children had. When he asked the friars where they might be, especially his mother, they shrugged their shoulders and answered, "In heaven, my boy, in heaven."

A rickety stairway led to the monastery storeroom and garret, where the friars warned Marcelino a tall man was hiding. The child was not to climb these stairs. But he did. He found the tall Man on a Cross. Day after day he visited Him, took Him a quilt to cover Him, took Him bread and wine to eat and even a bit of meat on a day it was permitted in the friary.

This day the Man came down from the Cross and sat at the poor table in the attic with Marcelino.

"Aren't you afraid of Me?" He asked the child.

"No," replied the boy.

"Do you know who I am?" the Man asked.

"Yes, You are God," said Marcelino.

Then Jesus told His little friend the story of His own childhood, His life, His death. He asked Marcelino about himself.

"My story," said the lad, "will not take long. I have no mother. You have a mother, haven't you?"

"Yes," Jesus answered.

"Where is she?" asked Marcelino.

"With yours," Jesus answered.

"And what are mothers like?" the child asked, this the supreme question of his short life. "I have always been thinking about mine and what I would like better than anything else would be to see her, if only for a moment." Then our Lord explained to him what mothers are like.

You are Marcelino, each one of you. You are all asking the question that he asked. You are asking the same Person. You are asking God, "What are mothers like?" Your vocation is motherhood. Your future is motherhood. This is the single, unique, perfect privilege of being a woman.

Those of you who know Part II of Goethe's *Faust* will remember the Mothers as the most mysterious, almost prophetic, of all the powers at work in the play.

For motherhood, in its widest, divinely providential functions, is the most profound of human destinies. One woman realized and fulfilled it perfectly. You will realize and fulfill it in terms of your own capacities, your free wills and your acceptances and responses to God's will, to grace. You will realize it spiritually, sacramentally, or vicariously. Whatever you do, whatever you are, you will do and be as a woman, and in one of these three tremendous vocations of womanhood.

Some of you, like Marcelino, will fall in love with the great Man on the Cross. You will ask to bathe His wounds, and to take the nails from His hands and feet. You will not be afraid of Him. You will know that He is God.

If you have the courage to climb the attic steps of quest and love you will find Him waiting for you. He will take the food and drink you bring Him. He will tell you about His mother. He will tell you what mothers are like. He will ask you to find the consummation of life in your mutual love. He will entrust to you the spiritual motherhood of hundreds of His children, His sick, His suffering, His lone and motherless ones. He will ask you to teach others the mysteries of His love. He may ask you to be sisters of His holy Cross.

The monks who cared for the foundling Marcelino did not go with him to the attic where he talked with God and knew His most intimate love. They stayed in the domestic area of their monastery. They cooked and cleaned and worked in the fields, pausing at times for prayer.

Most of you, unlike the monks, will mother, not foundlings, but your own children. You will be homemakers, housekeepers, delving, planting in the gardens of life with pauses at the day's beginning and end for prayer. Yours will be a sacramental motherhood, blessed and hallowed by the great sacrament of marriage.

Some of you will replace mothers in your own homes, or elsewhere in the special vocation of selfless dedication to others.

Your four years at college have not had as their objective the earning of 128 acceptable units of academic credit. These total a series of disciplines through which you have been trained intellectually to understand, to undertake, and to do the things that mothers must be able to do. They have taught you the dignity of obedience, the nobility of sacrifice, the sanctity of selflessness, the wonder of beauty, the joy of goodness, the freedoms of truth, the securities of faith, the sanities of hope, the divinity of love.

These do not look like the courses on your class cards, the curriculum in your college bulletin, but there are vital bonds between them, relations of cause and effect.

For fifteen, twenty years and more you have been eating three meals a day—breakfasts, lunches, and dinners. These do not look a bit like the girl, the young woman that you are. But, physically, they have produced very much of what you are. Analogically, your four years of arts and sciences do not look like you, but they, too, have produced much of what you are intellectually.

Both your physical and your intellectual selves find their highest fulfillment in your perfection as women. For that, you ask Marcelino's question, "What are mothers like?" Less fortunate than he, you cannot ask Christ directly, in such personal conversation as was his. But with unique congruity you ask the daughters of His suffering, the sisters of His holy Cross and their collaborators. Through them God will explain to you what mothers are like.

Even so prosaic an event as a college convocation may help you to see better both Mary, the mother of Jesus, and your college, the mother of your mind. Through the disciplines of your totaled A's and B's and C's you may realize the motherhood, spiritual, sacramental, vicarious for which God has created you.

X

We Work Our Way Through College

I WANT to talk to you today on the fact, the business, and the privilege of working your way through college. A number of our colleges deliberately set up programs to enable their students to earn much or all of their school expenses. I have Berea College in Kentucky and Antioch College, Yellow Springs, Ohio, particularly in mind. Generous and genuine teachers; earnest, industrious students; good creative arts and crafts result from such programs. No curriculum can offer a substitute for disciplined and intelligent work. No college can promise richer rewards than the rewards of honest, consistent work.

Certainly there is no college today without its well organized service program to help students finance their education. Let me illustrate by the best one of which I know. One girl in every ten earns part of her college education. One girl in every sixteen works her entire way through college. In addition to fulfilling academic requirements day after day she earns by service to the school at least fifteen hundred dollars every year to meet expenses of tuition and maintenance. Seven per cent of these students are on the honor roll. To this extent and financially we can and do work our way through college.

There are other and more inclusive ways of doing this. Indeed, the only way to get through college is to work one's way. The work that everyone must do is that specialized kind which we call study. Before we speak of it, let us consider work itself as a universal vocation, as a gift of God—almost His oldest gift to man. Our ability and our privilege to work are among the first and proudest signs of personal responsibility. Until we are six years old we play. Our companions are our playmates. Apart from food and sleep, life is just one game after another. By our sixth year we have become a bit restive under this lack of serious occupation and responsibility. We make our games matters of work. Even so, we are impatient to start to school, to begin our lifetime of work. That first day at school, in spite of various bewilderments, is among the proudest of our lives. It marks the end of our infancy and irresponsibility. Since then we have been persons committed to a life of work. The particular work for which and by which we are being trained here is school, college, study. Everything that we do for the rest of our active lives will have the qualities and the purposes of school, of study. Let us make no mistake about this. All our vacations, most of them much too long, much too overrun with workshops and other educational epidemics, have only one main purpose: to help us to do more and better work.

We not only work our way through school. We work our way through life. And the emptiest day of all our years will be the one in which we have to give up work for the last time; when we are retired because of age if we are professional persons; when we have to be waited on by our grandchildren if we are parents; when we move to an infirmary or a nursing home. We will learn to fill the subsequent days with the rich activities of meditation, reading, prayer. We will not be able to reclaim the zest, the joy of our whole being that is the best reward of legitimate work well done.

This, however, is running years ahead. Has it ever occurred

to you that the best things that men do and have done are always categorized as work? Greek architecture, Gothic cathedrals, our great museums and art galleries are all the works of masters. A musical composition carries the name, "opus." Opera is the glorification of work. We have the works of Aristotle, of Shakespeare. Our most highly organized sports have their strenuous workouts. On all levels, and particularly in our country, we are working animals. The poetic simile, "busy as a bee" can well give way to "busy as an American."

On the ultimate, the highest level we are children of God and about our Father's business. In any exegesis, the universe, existence itself began with the work of creation. That work is still in process: "The Father worked until now, and I work," Jesus said. As His adopted brothers, as Christians we are working with Him.

As Christian students we have this temporary four-year vocation to share the creative work of the Blessed Trinity through study. Our college life lasts only four years. For some of us, these years are all before us; for others, only the last year remains. But all of them have been given us to prepare harder, braver, more selfless, holier work. Let us begin the year knowing that this is a much more accurate description of our future than the college calendar or the football schedule. Let us begin it knowing that no other year in all our lives, nor indeed in all time, is important for us in the ways or for the reasons that this year is.

Going to college means going to work. This work involves our teachers, our books, our companions, our recreations, our parents, our selves, our Lady, and God. Some days ago, Connie Lou, aged seven, and her six-year-old cousin Bettina were in my office. Said Connie Lou to me, "Our teacher does two things at our school. One I like, the other I don't like. First, she tells us stories. Then she makes us work. I like the stories. I don't like the work." Said I to Connie Lou, "Perhaps some day when you grow up you may be a teacher, too. What will you do with your pupils? Will you tell them stories, or will you make them work?" With no shade of doubt or hesitance in her mind or in her answer, Connie replied, "I will make them work." "Make them work," affirmed Bettina relentlessly. Your teachers are all Connie Lous and Bettinas come of age. They are all of like mind. They mean to make you work. At least, I hope they do.

Then, there are your books. The other day I blew the dust off a volume on my bookshelf entitled "How To Read a Book." On page 110, Mortimer Adler says, "The most direct sign that you have done the work of reading is *fatigue*. . . . If you are not tired out you probably have not been doing the work. . . . It always was and still is the hardest work I do."

Obviously, your books expect you to work your way through college. My mother wrote in all our books, even texts in mathematics, "My books are my friends. Treat them kindly." I can never be reconciled to the all-but-universal practice of selling all of our textbooks, almost before our courses in them are ended. These books have shared some of the most formative and apocalyptic moments of our lives. Yet we are glad to part company with them for a few miserable pennies.

May I digress for a moment on this matter of books. Among the multitudes clamoring for attention as *musts* let us make a list—today is not too early—a list of the books that in our lives we can least afford not to know. Let us read again this list, no matter what the books-of-the-month may be. Then no matter what others are reading today and will have forgotten tomorrow we can say with disconcerting simplicity, "No, I haven't read *Advise and Consent*. But I have read all of the Bible, most of Plato and Dante and Chaucer, and all of Shakespeare." The book review groups will be rather impressed.

A second digression: I could pray that *The Kinsey Report* and books approximating its matter smelled. Every nose would surely reject what thousands of dubiously broad minds tolerate.

Our books are our friends in this business of working our way through college. They, with our teachers, are the intellectuals whose business is to make us work. Our other friends, our roommates, classmates, boy friends, blind dates, or visual aids, are about this same business as we are. So why not settle at the very beginning of the year for a mutual, reciprocal exchange of services in helping one another work our way through school?

Almost the first question asked when a student fails or gets behind in class or low in marks is, "Who are her friends?"

Our friends help make our recreations and our recreations help make our friends. Our choices in both require real wisdom, judgment, courage, strength of character. If we are serious in this business of work we can be immensely helpful to one another. We can work as well as play together and like it.

What shall we say about our parents? The day we were born they began working our way through school. We are all here now because they are working our way through college. They have spent sixteen, eighteen, twenty and more years working for the basic necessities for these four years that we spend so gaily and wish away with such impatient prodigality. Is there one among us who will not study her way through school with all her might in merest gratitude?

At last we have come to ourselves, the workers. Are we in love with work, its wonder, its dignity, its worthiness? Have we ever watched for a long time the washing of the waves upon a shore, the hurrying of a brook to its brother river, the tireless turbulence of a waterfall? All ceaselessly working; all beautiful in their work. Have we stood and looked and listened to the hushed and breathless busyness of dawn, working the tremendous wonder of a new day? Have we seen from year to year the young sapling at its proper work of making a great tree? Our world is filled with these wonderworkers. Without a coke, without a cigarette, without a voice over the radio, or face on the TV, they are all at work making the physical world. We will agree that they do a beautiful job.

Finally, let us see ourselves working our way through college. Our proper work is study. Study has been described as a prayer to truth. As college students and teachers we are consecrated to truth. We are lovers of truth as philosophers are lovers of wisdom. Shall we set a measure to this love? Are we willing to die for the truth? At least, are we willing to live for it? Let me quote this last perfect reason which includes all others:

"Jesus Christ needs our minds for His work, as on earth He needed His own human mind. He has gone, but we continue Him; we have that measureless honor. We are His 'members,' therefore have a share in His spirit, are therefore His co-operators. He acts outwardly through us, and inwardly through the inspirations of His Spirit, as in His lifetime He acted outwardly by His voice, inwardly by His grace. Our work being a necessary part of that action, let us work as Jesus meditated—as He drew on the life-springs of the Father to pour them out on the world."

For this we work our way through college, work that is a prayer for truth, a vocation, a transfiguration. Two thousand years ago a little Boy of twelve looked into the face of the Mother of God and asked, "Did you not know that I must be about my Father's business?" Every girl, every teacher is in a sense that perennial child, looking into the face of that Mother. We must be about our Father's business. The Father worked until now and we work.

XI

The Right to Truth in Education

THE right to teach supernatural truth is our greatest human right in education. To exercise this right we must have proper training. We must study theology. Time was, half a century ago, when the preamble of our constitution summarized neatly and succinctly for us our essential human rights: life, liberty, the pursuit of happiness. That was before liberty had become so carefully broken down and the pursuit of happiness so carelessly broken up.

The science of ethics then was much simpler than it is today. Our rights were not in such an inextricable tangle. Our duties and responsibilities were not held in abeyance or rejected. Education itself, without the dazzling material perfections of modern plant equipment and the relentless application of standardized theories, had somehow managed to attend to first things. What validity there is in our present intellectual life testifies in a large measure to the correctness, the soundness of our pre-Dewey training. Educators are not without misgivings as to what legacy these middle years of our century are preparing for its end. They find little reassurance in the prevailing confusions, the present conflicts between human rights and education. I should like to consider a most fundamental right in education and in life itself, our right to truth. Perhaps by stating some aspects of this right we can come to a better understanding of it. We may defend it more actively; we may exercise it more fearlessly.

The human rights involved in education that are on the tops of our minds at the moment are chiefly material ones: rights to transportation, to free textbooks on nonreligious subjects, to milk or lunches, to health service. The rights to released time for instruction in religion and to the use of our schoolrooms for such instruction transcend the purely material.

In these fields, however, any human rights that we should possess have passed into the domain of local, state, or federal legislation. Whether or not we like these appropriations we must accept them. For years we have watched the usurpation of human rights by human mights: the might of power, of money, of propaganda, of prejudice, of pseudopsychology. Perhaps we are helpless against all these. Perhaps we are cowardly or apathetic. Perhaps we are too ignorant, too unsure of our position and our essential rights to defend them. Perhaps we are unwilling to suffer and to die for them. Whatever the cause we are not going to correct them at the moment. We are going to consider a human right of which we are depriving ourselves.

Most of us have grown up with the conviction that we have a right to our opinions. I remember a very keen-minded teacher who used to insist: "You haven't a right to your opinion. You have a right to the truth."

The Christian school rests on these statements of Christ, one a promise, one a command: "You shall know the truth and the truth shall make you free," and "Go, therefore, and teach all nations. . . . Go into the whole world and preach the gospel to every creature." This command to teach the whole world establishes our supernatural human right to Christian schools and to Christian education. They establish our duty to become Christian teachers, our duty to teach the

truth, the science of God to all the world. The Catholic school
is not an optional institution. It is founded to fulfill this duty
to teach, to protect this right to truth. This is the age of science. In an age of science or in any other age the function and
essential right of the Catholic school is to teach the science
of God and to integrate with it all other science, all other
knowledge on all the various levels of learning and of teaching.

Perhaps here we should establish the place of theology or
the science of God as a practical science. A science is practical
in so far as it leads to a useful end. The better the end, the
better the science. Man has always asked: "Why am I living?
To whom am I absolutely responsible? Does my existence end
with death?" These questions and their true answers are the
most important in human existence. Theology is the only
science that answers them with certitude. Obviously it is the
most practical as it is the noblest of sciences. Now we must
take theology, like Mary's lamb, to school.

This may not seem to be a great human right to us, but it
is. We are almost the only teachers in the Western world who
are free to exercise it. We are free to teach our students the
truth of the existence of God, the Incarnation, the Redemption, their own supernatural destiny. We are free to open
and to read to them God's letters, the books of the Sacred
Scriptures. We are free to instruct them in the tradition of
Christianity, in the history of the Church. We are free to do
all this, but are we prepared?

Before answering this question, let us ask another. Who are
these students upon whom we are exercising this right to
truth, to the science of God? They are its legitimate heirs.
They are the children of God. They come to us first in the
state of baptismal innocence, a condition which entitles them
immediately, should they die thus, to the Beatific Vision. As
sensible teachers we cannot undertake our right to teach truth
to such pupils without the most adequate knowledge and

the greatest reverence. Our teaching must be a sublimated pedagogy and we can approach it only with profoundest awe.

During their first seven years these children of God participate in some of the greatest possible human experiences including birth and baptism. They go to confession. They kneel at the feet of God, personally, orally to tell Him that they have offended Him, to ask and to receive His forgiveness. Most of them will never appear in a civil court. All of them, by the time they are eight years old, have had the spiritual maturity and the august experience of standing alone as culprits before the high court of God. They have all had the experience of receiving full pardon for their offenses. These pupils of ours during these first years with us have assisted intelligently at the Sacrifice of the Mass. They have been sacramentally in dialogue with Christ in the supper room at Jerusalem and on Mount Calvary at His death. As truly as the apostles, they have listened to His words of consecration, have received His Body and Blood. These are tremendous events, skyscraping experiences. We have helped to prepare our boys and girls for them.

Today our minds are full of training for national and international defense. The Catholic child is inducted into the army of Christ before he is twelve. He has put on the armor of God. The pentecostal winds envelop him. The Holy Spirit inflames him with its divine gifts and fruits. He is marked forever as a Christian, strengthened and confirmed, a soldier of Jesus Christ. We have given him at least a part of his military training.

Briefly, these are the spiritual experiences and qualifications that we share with our children through the elementary grades. Our sharing has been by way of an elementary theology. Our curricula call for physical science, social science; but the integrating science is theology, the science of God. What if, on this level, we call it religion. If we teach truth every subject, however profane, must be luminous from its relation to the science of God. I know that this ideal is not easily realized. I know that it must be if schools are ever to become truly catholic.

Through secondary departments we continue to share with our students their extended human right to education, their supernatural human right to the knowledge of God. Their great sacramental experiences should continue with regularity. A deepened spiritual life and sensitivity should be the result. During these years the permanent pattern of manhood and womanhood is made. We help to make it. Often, under God, ours is a determining influence. Our students must know the truth through our presentation of it. It must be patent in every lesson they study, in every game they play, if they are to bring an integrated Christian manhood and womanhood to their world.

On the college level the student is prepared to study theology itself and to see its close and necessary relation to every other field of knowledge. The thoughtful students will realize that it is the noblest of all sciences and that if they wish to dedicate their minds to truth, this is the perfect subject of their election. Nowhere have we a more beautiful, a more opportune moment to exercise our right to truth in education than with our college students, and nowhere are we so ill prepared.

Our youth today, outside of Catholic colleges and even in them, are spiritually illiterate and spiritually starved. A polio epidemic terrifies us into immediate and expert action. This wide-spread and growing epidemic of spiritual atrophy and deformity among our finest young men and women calls for all that we can do in and through the Holy Spirit of truth for its prevention, its cure. Our lack of great leaders today may be the result of our flagrant failure to teach religion as it should be taught. The Catholic leaders whom we do have are so largely because of the integrated catholicity of their minds and training. The strong department of theology in college, the fully trained, strong teacher of theology in college should be great parts of the exercise of our right to truth. The results will be a release of something beyond atomic energy. It will be a release of the omnipotence of God, acting through us, His teachers and His students.

I have tried to say that a number of human rights in education have been denied or withdrawn from us through prejudice, propaganda, law; that our supernatural right to truth, to the teaching of truth through theology, and of integrating this with profane truth is still ours. I have tried to indicate the aptitudes of our students on primary, secondary, and college levels for their participation in truth.

Now I come to the sequel which is in part the story of our failure, in part a plea for improvement. All over the world today, and in Catholic countries most of all, people have lost their human rights in education, their right to truth, their right to supernatural truth. We still have these. If we do not enjoy them to the full it is our own fault. We have deprived ourselves, and we continue to deprive ourselves of them.

Our Catholic schools were founded specifically to protect these rights. This means that their strongest departments should be their departments of theology, that their best teachers should be their teachers of theology. It means that everything else in their curricula and program should be correlated with theology.

I need not tell you that this is not so. Their greatest development has been in provision for natural truth, for the physical and social sciences, for laboratories, libraries, visual aids, recreation centers, athletic fields. No comparable development has taken place in the departments of theology and their faculties. Our schools, practically without exception, seek first the kingdom of accrediting agencies and their justice. Our teachers, practically without exception, qualify first to meet state educational requirements. They acquire, at all costs and sacrifices, their credits in their major and minor teaching fields in secular knowledge. After all these things do the heathens seek.

Would any principal or dean or president assign a class in biology or chemistry or political science to a teacher who had had no training beyond the experience of living in an age of science? We do not act on the assumption that because we speak the English language we can teach college or high school or even elementary English, that because we are Americans we are even the poorest kind of teachers of American history. Yet all of our lives our Catholic schools have operated on the assumption that because we are Catholics and teachers we can teach theological truth.

This is, I think, our greatest misunderstanding and sin against our greatest human right in education, our right to teach supernatural truth. Not our laws, not our enemies, we ourselves, we religious and lay educators are depriving ourselves of this essential liberty.

I will not say that much is not being done to correct this. But of all fields of Catholic education, this is the one in which the greatest, best, most sustained work must be done. It is neither presumptuous nor Utopian to say that it can be done. It is only Catholic to say that it must and will be done. Having met so many less worthy, less glorious, more onerous issues for the sake of secular demands, we can meet this for God's sake.

In exercising our right to teach supernatural truth, theology, we integrate our entire curricula so that all knowledge will lead to God and God will lead to all knowledge. To understand this effectively is to understand our most vital human right in education. To achieve it is to be a Christian teacher.

XII

Would You Like to Study Theology?

EDUCATION has three very hot irons in the fire at the moment. The first is increasing enrollments everywhere. The second is development programs and the needs for financial aid. The third has been in the fire longest. For this and other reasons it is probably the hottest. It is the iron of religion in education.

Public schools exist to teach secular knowledge. By law, they are Christian schools only because they exist in the Christian era, in the year of Our Lord.

The Catholic school has for the reason of its being the teaching of Christian doctrine. It would willingly leave to the public school its proper fields of profane knowledge and devote its time and other resources to the teaching of theology, of sacred doctrine. In the United States such a program has not proved feasible. The Catholic school, in consequence, carries the double responsibility of instruction in both profane and sacred truth.

The program of secular knowledge is highly organized and protected by regulations, standards, and requirements. Teachers in Catholic schools, in order to meet these standards, have fulfilled and will continue to fulfill all the requirements necessary to make them fully qualified secular teachers. The teaching of religion, under whatever title, is not and cannot be a part of these standard educational requirements. Consequently, no standard for teacher preparation in this field is set up and, sadly enough, none is fulfilled.

Our three greatest privileges are birth, baptism, and death. Once we are successfully born our biggest business is to make a perfect success of dying. All that fills the interval called life is some form of education. Baptism is our induction and our first great lesson. Most of us learn the realities of this lesson years later. Our whole life can be spent in studying, understanding, loving, and living these. Until we open the beautiful door of death we shall not realize completely the meaning of this, the first experience of our Christian life. First grade children are baptized children still in the state of baptismal innocence. Nurses will examine their bodies; teachers will test their mental attitudes. Can teachers without a basic training in theology meet these children on a proper spiritual altitude?

In the great panorama of elementary education the existence of God, the Trinity, the Incarnation, Mary, the sacraments shine out. What orthodox formation and information do our programs for the preparation of teachers provide for these? They require the study of child psychology in order that our children may be taught as human beings. Teachers should study fundamental theology in order to teach their pupils as children of God.

The study of theology also implies the study of the sacred scriptures. The critics of Christ reproached Him for teaching the scriptures without having studied them. What can be said of our responsibility to study and to understand in order to teach them correctly? If, through the incompetence of a teacher, a child learns to spell, to read, to multiply incorrectly, the error is serious and regrettable. If, through lack of instruction on the part of the teacher, the child fails to know and love and serve God, fails to enter into his great Christian heritage, the error reaches far beyond the range of pedagogy. Jesus may have had our teachers of Christian Doctrine in mind when He said, "Suffer the little children to come to me." They come largely through their teachers.

This unpublished story of Gilbert K. Chesterton establishes the level on which the minds of the child and the wise man meet in the field of theology. The Catholic priest of Beaconsfield, England, was sitting in his study one rainy evening when he heard a knock at the door. Beaconsfield was the home of the G. K. Chestertons. The pastor had never met them.

Opening the door, he found himself face to face with the big man of the town. Ushering him into the study and inviting him to be seated, Father asked:

"Is there something that I can do for you, Mr. Chesterton?"

"Yes, Father," came the quick reply. "You can perform the greatest act of charity that one person can do for another. You can teach me the truth."

"You mean that you want me to instruct you to become a Catholic."

"Yes, Father, I do."

In his amazement Father made this quick mental survey of the situation: "Twenty miles from here, at Oxford, are Martin D'Arcy and Ronald Knox, and he asks me to instruct him!" Aloud, he simply asked:

"Are you sure you want me to instruct you?"

"Yes," came the Chestertonian reply. "When I am a Catholic you will be the most important person in my life. You will be my pastor. I want you to instruct me."

"How would you like to begin?" asked the still astonished pastor.

Again the perfect Chestertonian answer:

"I want to enter the kingdom of heaven. Our Lord has said that unless we become as little children we cannot enter the kingdom of heaven. How would you instruct a little child?"

"I would give him the little catechism," was Father's quick answer.

"Good! Have you got one?" from the great catechumen.

Father handed him one from the pile on the table. Chesterton leafed through the first pages to the questions:

"Who made you?"

"Why did God make you?"

"The answers to these questions are what the whole world is seeking," he said simply as he began his first catechism lesson.

The great essayist, philosopher, poet reasserts so confidently Our Lord's request and our own plea for theological training. The little catechism should be taught as theology and not as a series of memory exercises. Not only Chesterton, but hundreds of non-Catholic university students read it avidly.

Boys and girls in their teens are just beginning to face problems of good and evil, suffering, the great laws of life, the majestic realities which, to quote Keats, "tease us out of thought as doth eternity." These boys and girls in an age of science need to be answered in terms of the queen of sciences, theology.

Let us take a look at a typical college student receiving a typical college education. One hot October evening the president of a Midwest college for women met a senior on her way to dinner.

"I am so tired," she said. "We have been working all afternoon in the laboratory on an embalmed cat."

The girl was pretty, fastidious, intelligent. If she had been required to spend half the afternoon in a class in theology, she would probably have been bored; she might have protested. The mysteries of God were not absorbing to her. The embalmed cat was.

In a trice, the president made an evaluation in weights and measures. Here was a typical student, two subject matters, two teachers. There could be no question of the comparative excellence of subjects, God and the embalmed cat. The teacher of theology was probably not properly prepared. The biology teacher was the finest professor on the campus.

Within the year a graduate program in theology was set up, staffed, and functioning on that campus. A number of the best teachers on the faculty were assigned to study the sacred scriptures and theology; in fact to qualify for doctor's degrees in philosophy with these subjects for their majors and minors. The reason was not that the president and faculty valued the embalmed cat less, but that they valued God and the proper study of Him more.

The best person to explain the meaning of a great book to us is its author. The best person to interpret a great work of art is the master artist. The best person to reveal to us the wonders of atomic energy is the creator of atomic energy. God has written the book of the world for us, has created the masterpiece of the world for us, has brought the atom and its tremendous potentials into being. The more we know and understand and love Him in all of His being and activities, the more completely we can enter into every aspect of the world and of all existence.

Let us realize of what spirit we are. This is the age of the Holy Spirit. The winds of Pentecost are sweeping the world. We are, or can be, again in the upper room of the Cenacle. The parted tongues of theology, of Sacred Scriptures may rest upon our heads. We may study and teach all truth against the background of inspired truth, theology, the science of God.

XIII

The Sky Is Not the Limit

You may remember a childhood story of the little prince who cried for the moon. His distraught nurse finally thought to give him a mirror in which he caught the reflected satellite. The story is now. We are all crying for the moon and reaching for the stars. The quest is perennial, very old, very new. It exists in our most ancient myths, our newest laboratories.

Until a decade ago the sky was our physical limit. It will never be so again. Within your life span you may well be moving among planets as, until now, men have moved among continents. Pioneers from your generation may have climbed hundreds of miles into space, may be exploring our satellite, the moon. Without traveling any farther from the earth than Washington is from New York, they may have broken through our atmospheric smog, and come out into the amazing clarity of Mars.

The planetary universe is perhaps nearer and more accessible to your generation than the Western Hemisphere was to the world of Columbus and Isabella. You must have something to do with its destiny as it will have with yours. We will do well to consider these certitudes.

Arthur C. Clarke in *Horizons* for January, 1959, writes:

"Astronomy is the oldest of the sciences and the one that has not only the widest popular appeal but also the most profound philosophical implications. This was never more true than at the present time, when the horizons of human knowledge are not so much expanding as exploding. . . .

"In a period that will be very short by the standards of history—perhaps a century at the most—we may have established physical contact with all the major solid bodies in our solar system. A landing on the remotest of the sun's planets may now be nearer to us in time than the Battle of Gettysburg.

"The shadow of these coming events already lies across our age, stirring the thoughts of all men who have ever stared at the night sky and wondered what part our species is destined to play in the unfolding drama of the universe. Many of the great questions of religion and philosophy must now be reformulated, and there is more than a possibility that some which seemed forever beyond hope of solution may soon be answered."

Suppose we move forward by moving backward. Astronomy has kept age-old company with fairy lore, nursery rhymes, myth, literature, revelation. As children we climbed into the sky with Jack in the Beanstalk. The story is a true one, as is the moral. The adventure as an experience is partly yours, partly before you. However much you know of it, now or later, you cannot tell of it more gaily than Edna St. Vincent Millay did forty years ago. In her poem, "The Beanstalk," she writes:

> Ho, Giant! This is I!
> I have built me a beanstalk into your sky!
> La,—but it's lovely, up so high!
> . . .
> What a wind! What a morning!—
> . . .

Your broad sky, Giant,
Is the shelf of a cupboard;
I make beanstalks, I'm
A builder, like yourself,
But beanstalks is my trade,
I couldn't make a shelf,
Don't know how they're made,
Now, a beanstalk is more pliant—
La, what a climb!

Jack's sky was full of golden treasure, all of which he brought back home to his Mother Earth. Then, wiser than most buccaneers, he cut down the beanstalk and killed the treasure-greedy giant of the skies. What a wise boy was he!

Jack was not a solitary explorer of the heavens.

There was an old woman
Went up in a basket
Fifty times as high as the moon
Where she was going
I could not but ask it
For in her hand
She held a long broom.
"Old woman, old woman, old woman,"
    quoth I,
"Where are you going? You're flying so high."
"To sweep all the cobwebs out of the sky,
I will be back again by and by."

As of now, she has not returned. She must have got rather quickly into orbit. Her astronomical distance interests us, fifty times as high as the moon, also her housewifely care to clear away the atmospheric wrappings about our earth.

Jack and his beanstalk may or may not be prophetic of our space climbers. This remarkable woman in her basket may or may not suggest analogies for the biblical woman of the third chapter of Genesis and the woman of the Apocalypse. Having been promised by God in His ultimatum to the Devil, "I will put enmity between thee and the woman" she is a very old woman. St. John's vision, "a woman clothed with the sun, the moon under her feet and upon her head a crown of twelve stars" leaves no place for cobwebs in the firmament, for transcendent womanhood in a transcendent universe. Young women completing their collegiate preparations for life in the universe may find these analogies are provocative. For these women of prophecy and of nursery rhymes, the sky was not the limit.

This may all seem gratuitous and farfetched. It happens that Old King Cole was the father of Saint Helena; that Little Jack Horner and his family are of historic English gentry. Other nursery rhymes may imply more than meets the eye. God has never left Himself without witnesses. He has conditioned our qualities for entrance into His household on the literal or acquired simplicities of childhood. May we not rest our faith in the implication of nursery rhymes as such evidence?

Even our domestic animals have abandoned themselves with something like euphoria to space travel. For how many generations of children has "the cow jumped over the moon"? Happier than his contemporary canines, "the little dog laughed" at such bovine lunacy.

Air travel and domestication on the planets take us into centuries preceding our nursery rhymes. The myths of the Western world seek out their heroes, stellify them, place them in the constellations and among the stars that still bear their names.

Apart from the deities, Jupiter, Mars, Venus, and the rest, we look up night after night to the starry belt of Orion, the chair of Cassiopeia; the twins, Castor and Pollux. The animal world shared easy metamorphosis in mythology and found equal paths to glory among the stars. The Bears and Capella, the goat; Draco, the dragon; Leo, the majestic lion are only a few that we all know by starlight.

Contemporary astronomy is of quite a different complexion. It will be long, however, before we match the compassionate and superhuman daring of Prometheus. To relieve the bleak and frigid lot of men, this Titan stole fire from the sun and brought it in a hollow reed to earth. Its heat and warmth and cheer have ever since made the happiness of men the envy of the gods.

Daedalus and his son Icarus, most skillful artisans but mere men for all that, fashioned wings of wax and feathers by which the boy transcended the heights of the heavens. In his air-intoxication he flew too near the sun, the wax wings melted and he fell into the sea and drowned.

Prometheus was a semigod. Icarus was merely human. The one achieved the sun. The other died in the quest. The myths testify to the unknown gods of antiquity. They may foreshadow our story.

Scriptures and Revelation take us into the realms of truth and faith. Here, in the very infancy of historic man, we are told of Henoch who walked with God and was seen no more among men. His assumption elicits no question and no doubt from the inspired writer of the Book of Genesis.

The Book of Kings, with equal historicity, states that the Prophet Elias was taken up to heaven, dropping his mantle upon his disciple Eliseus. The ascension of Jesus and the assumption of Mary, while properly matters of Sacred History and doctrinal definition, lift the cumulative testimony of man's possession of the air, his penetration into space to supernatural heights and validity. God as Man and the Son of a human mother found the avenues of air and space no strangers to Himself. He found them congruous and fit for His mother. As His sons and daughters, we may with reverence and joy and wonder follow Them.

Once at least in its history architecture attempted a structural beanstalk. The Tower of Babel, a fiasco in construction, resulted in a confusion of the tongues of its builders. It marks the beginning of a multitude of languages that are still the basis of verbal communication. This may happen again if men find rational beings on Mars, let us say, unlike us in physique; unlike us, too, in their means of communication. Have you ever thought of this, ever wondered?

Our earth and our heavens cannot have been so full of this celestial trafficking without great reflections in literature. The greatest is, of course, Dante's *Divine Comedy*. While essentially a spiritual odyssey, it employs the astronomical setting and theory of his day. Following him Chaucer, in his *Troilus and Criseyde,* discovers his hero, slain in battle, viewing from the planet Mercury "this litel spot of erthe, that with the se embraced is." But both the Italian and the English poets found in their empyreans God's will as their peace.

Years ago, Jules Verne used to register great indignation at finding his books on the shelves of juvenile reading in American libraries. We know now how right he was. Twenty and more years ago, C. S. Lewis, English philosopher, novelist, essayist, wrote two books that can be reread slowly and thoughtfully today. *Out of the Silent Planet* is the story of two English space travelers who reached Mars. Here they came upon a population of rational beings, unlike men in appearance, living under a government resembling, in outline, Plato's Republic. They were an unfallen race. Evil had never touched them. The facts and results of Original Sin did not exist.

The visitors to Mars were graciously received and entertained. Among other amenities, they were taken out to fish while they were awaiting word from the ruler of Mars to be presented to him. Just as one lucky fisherman was pulling in his catch, the imperial summons came. The fisherman said, "Just wait until I land this fish." The entire island shuddered;

the inhabitants sickened at the only moment of imperfect obedience that had ever occurred on the planet.

Let this one instance stand for the two volumes presenting a world free from Original Sin, and in *Perelandra,* a world wrested from evil by the redeeming passion of the protagonist and his incomparable love.

The quest of the air reaches far beyond the possibilities, the potencies of science. It raises such questions as C. S. Lewis has presumed.

Is man the only rational mortal being?
Is there a sinless world of such beings,
or more than one?

Many years ago, Alice Meynell in her poem, "Christ in the Universe," wrote:

With this ambiguous earth
His dealings have been told us. These abide:
The signal to a maid, the human birth,
The lesson, and the young Man crucified.
But not a star of all
The innumerable host of stars has heard
How He administered this terrestrial ball.
Our race have kept their Lord's entrusted Word.
. . .
Nor, in our little day,
May His devices with the heavens be guessed,
His pilgrimage to thread the Milky Way,
Or His bestowals there be manifest.

But in the eternities
Doubtless we shall compare together, hear
A million alien Gospels, in what guise
He trod the Pleiades, the Lyre, the Bear.

O, be prepared, my soul,
To read the inconceivable, to scan
The million forms of God those stars unroll
When, in our turn, we show to them a Man.

The places in this universe are more plausible now for you
than America was for youth in 1492. Have your years at college helped you to dare and to bear your future, to be used
by God as Columbus was, to be a Christ-bearer, a dove?
The inhabitants of other worlds are not looking for us.
At least no report of them has come. Why? Are their worlds
so much more perfect? Are they living in boundless space,
in infinity? Has eternity begun for them? Again I quote from
Arthur Clarke: "The Roman Catholic Church has already
accepted and welcomed the coming of the space age. In 1956
the International Astronautical Federation held a congress in
Rome and heard an address from the Pope in which he ex-
pressed the view that, now that man had discovered the means
of exploring the universe, God clearly intends him to use
it. This is a teaching which most men, whatever their be-
liefs, will surely accept. Any path to knowledge is a path to
God."
To the universe and its wonders your college commits you.
Aristotle used to say that "all men begin wondering why
things are as they are." We have scarcely begun to guess,
much less to know that they are as they are. We have begun
to wonder. We do know that the sky is not the limit.
Your generation is committed to the quest of space and
outer space as children of men. C. S. Lewis says, "Our loyalty
is due not to our species but to God." Suppose that our science-
driven world had given itself to the quest of the God of space,
to His infinity, to His eternity. In what a transfigured world
we would be living! You are living, and have been living
in such a world. You must continue to do so.
Will you move with me now from the areas of natural to

supernatural air travel? The simplest, most familiar of such airways is prayer.

Every time you say "Our Father" you have transcended time and space. Every time you say "Hail Mary" you have moved into the immortal and supernatural areas of human existence. Every time you say a litany, or any real prayer, you have passed beyond the boundaries of merely natural human experience. You have shared the exhilarations of contact with perfections unlimited. You return from your superstellar journey, revitalized, recharged with supernatural life. Your flight has been surrounded by no life hazards, has entailed no tragic casualties. You return to your temporal world with confirmations of every promise made to men that we are now the children of God and it has not yet appeared what we shall be.

Let us return to our fairy stories, our nursery rhymes. Since the infancy of the human race, the children of men have been creeping on the floor of their home, the earth. After long centuries that will be moments in cosmic life, some of them have grown up enough to stand alone, to venture out into the yard of the bigger world, the universe, the everywhere. You are among these brave young boys and girls. You are the first generation in this age of stupendous change.

Buy yourselves bags of beans. Plant them, raise beanstalks. Let them grow to the highest heavens. Climb to their tops. Bring back the wealth of the universe that you discover. But cut down the beanstalks before the giant of greed and exploitation discovers and destroys you. Spend your lives in sharing your riches and in the joy of your great adventures into whatever spaces your beanstalks take you.

Keep intact a basket and a broom. On a day you will fly away to sweep all of the cobwebs out of the sky. You will never return. Your basket is faith. Your broom is love. Not science but the God of science will put you into orbit.

XIV

The Fabulous Wings

To YOU who have not yet had your eighteenth birthdays the
world today is normal. This generation is the only one you
have ever known, have ever lived in. You are completely con-
temporaneous. Even those of us who have had our fortieth
birthdays have never lived in a decade of peace. Wars and
rumors of wars have been our environment, our national
and international state of being. They have fashioned our
thinking. Our thinking has led us into areas never before
accessible to men.

Fifty years ago we were terrestrial bipeds. Now we are
highly rational birds, intrepid aquatics. Our quest of outer
space has just begun. The question, "How far can we go?"
may become in the year 2000, "Where shall we stop?"

Most of you will be amused to think that in 1900 the automobile was a much more primitive vehicle than the first
airplane that you ever saw. Think what air exploration can
become in another fifty years! The world of the deep seas—
the mountains, plains, rivers, valleys of the ocean floor—
may well, in that same time, become main traveled roads
for men. Tremendous enterprises are already busy on them.
We are not concerned at the moment with the conquests of
either of these greater worlds by us pedestrians on our own

small planet. Our earth is after all only a series of relatively big and little surfaces emerging from the great world of water into the greater world of air.

Our penetration into both of these worlds we regard as wonderful, as almost frightening—fabulous, to use the adjective of the moment. We have considered ourselves so long as earth-bound that we think of sky and sea as the proper possessions of birds and fish. We even felt a bit strange upon our first invasions of the proper elements of other forms of life.

But, after all, why should we not fly? Why should we not deep-sea dive? As men, we may be children of earth and nothing more. But we are not limited to our humanity. We are now the children of God, and it has not yet appeared what we shall be. Ultimately we shall have the supernatural properties of splendor, subtlety, agility. We shall be able to penetrate matter, to encompass distance with the immediacy of thought. Even now, in our approximations to omnipresence, we are revealing our lineage, we are seeking our spiritual homeland. In our most far-reaching quests of science we are following the call of the spirit—deep calls unto deep.

These things being so, we are more normal in traversing the heights and depths between which we live than in remaining imprisoned between them. No other beings try to do these things. We are God's only rational children on this our planet; truant children at times, lost children at times, but always His, immortally, eternally His, and gravitating back to Him. Perhaps we are nearer Him in this fantastic age than we have ever been. Perhaps we are finding our way through the conquest of the natural to the supernatural. There must be a point at which they meet. We may be nearer to it than we guess.

Just think what the next several decades may unfold! I use the threadbare expressions as terms of direct address, almost of command. Let us wonder; let us think; let us stop swallowing the universe like a pill. The English poet William Davies asks:

What is this life, if full of care
We have no time to stand and stare?

I invite you to a life of wonder, a life of thinking, a life in which often and often we will take time to stand and stare.

Our enterprise is one of mystery, of intimate intellectual companionship. We shall share the most delicate of human relationships, the marriage of true minds. We shall transfer from mind to mind these great spiritual entities: thoughts, ideas, ideals, inspirations. We shall participate in the greatest of all charities, the giving and receiving of truth.

As teachers, we bring to you our students these transcendental fruits of our lives. You, our students, bring your receptive, eager minds, your time, your youth, your folded futures, the wonder of yourselves, the capacities of which only God can measure.

Apart from Holy Communion, this communion of teacher and student is the most completely spiritual of all human relations. It is the sacrament of the intellectual life. Let us share it at its highest levels, the levels of theology and philosophy. Let us share it at the levels of poetry.

By definition, "Poetry is the divination of the spiritual in the things of sense." It is seeing things from God's point of view. John Dewey once wrote: "We agree that we are uncertain as to where we are going and where we want to go, and why we are doing what we do." Was there ever a recipe of folly more surely designed to ensure destruction? Education, under the shadow of the Sputnik, must seek the goal and the constant star—must know the whence, the whither, and the why, and must put vision before all else. Its motto must be that of the great Plato: "Education is to turn the eye of the soul toward light."

Education has tried many correctives, has sought many panaceas, has followed the light of many will-o'-the-wisps. At the moment it is recovering from the hypnoses of progressive education, of life adjustment, of togetherness. It has become eclectic and precocious on Great Books. It has fine-combed its conscience in self-studies. It has gone abroad. It has stayed at home. It has built laboratories for the sciences, the arts. It has tried religious emphasis. It has not tried poetry.

The poets are the mendicant minstrels, the orphan Annies in education. We have forgotten the word of the wise man, "When vision fails the nation perishes." We have forgotten that the poet is the seer, the maker, the singer. We have forgotten that the ages of greatest poetry, of epic poetry were ages of historic war or post-war. These things being so, now is the acceptable time. Now is the day of our intellectual salvation. Mayhap that salvation may come, in part at least, through the young poets now in college, as yet unrevealed as poets even to themselves.

Christopher Fry says in his *Sleep of Prisoners,* written in this precise setting:

> O God, the fabulous wings unused
> Folded in the heart.

I speak to you as possessors of these fabulous wings. I speak to you as teachers of our winged youth, our generation of poets, seers, and singers, the youth of a generation whose quest is exploration into God where no nation's foot, no student's, no teacher's has trodden yet.

On a summer boat from Detroit to Duluth a young college student, Michael, had charge of the dining room. Two young priests on board used to give Michael a few lines of poetry every day to identify. The game stirred the minds of many of the guests more than the food that was served. The best of all the poems was this, from *The Lady of the Lake:*

> Speed, Malise, speed! The dun deer's hide
> On fleeter foot was never tied.
> Speed, Malise, speed!

This is our song for flight into the infinite heights and depths of our own minds mutually shared this year. We are all poets in our capacities for sharing, if not in the making of songs.

Some years ago the president of the University of Notre Dame, Father Charles O'Donnell, built this house of beauty to which I invite you.

Design for a House

In my love, I would build you a house.
Its north wall will be God,
Its south wall will be God,
East and west you shall be walled with God.
You will need to fear no storms from the north,
Your south wall will be a sunny wall.
Dawn will stand for you, a wall of ivory growing into gold,
Your west wall will be a pearl, on fire.

Walk to the north wall forever, you will not reach it,
You will never stroke with your hands the arras that streams
    down the southern side;
Run eastward, infinitely, dawn will be still beyond you,
And you will be footsore indeed before ever your travel stop
    at the starred west wall.

In my love I would give you liberty, confining you only in
    the Infinite,
I would wall you up in the beauty of God,
In the reach and range of God.
I can think of nothing better I could do for you
Than build you a house, out of my love.

This can well be the design for your college as we build it with and for you.

XV

Teacher Education and Abiding Values

A GENERATION ago such a group of educators might well have been considering teacher training and basic technics. The years have shown us that these, narrowly interpreted, are not enough. Our horizons are all but boundless; our purposes are reaching out to everlasting ends. Our teachers must be not only trained in skills and technics; they must be educated in the great world of ideas and ideals, the abiding values of life.

We know the technics. Are these the abiding values in your education? If not, what are?

Some time ago in a group of college teachers, all younger than myself and representing widely different training and experience, I asked this question. Now I am asking each one of you: What are the abiding values in your education, your learning experience from kindergarten through graduate school?

Every teacher in the group began her answer with a reference to her teachers: "One teacher I shall never forget," "My best teacher," "The teacher who changed my life," and so on. I dare say that each of us can think of and answer silently for at least one great and memorable teacher.

Next in order of importance, my little group listed class-mates, schoolmates, fellow-students. They spoke of classes and subject matter only because the unforgettable teacher had made his subject unforgettable. From their consideration of abiding values in their education this group made no reference at all to their majors, minors, fields of concentration and specialization. Incidentally, these happened to range from theology to commerce, from biology to economics.

You must suspect that I am moving towards a moral. You are quite right. You have already guessed the moral. The teacher remains the abiding value in education. This being so, and I think that you agree that it is, teacher education must focus clearly and magnificently on developing the teacher as a person as well as a teacher. I hope that you agree with this order. Comes the question: How can this be done? The process is slow, is enigmatic, is altogether mysterious. Many factors can contribute. I shall suggest these: the factor of great books, and through books great ideas; the factor of language, the factor of life itself.

We are in an intellectual world of great books. Because of its magnitude it has become for most of us a wilderness. We need someone to help us find our way out, to choose a few from the bewildering number of possibilities. I have selected a dozen great books on which to rest the education of young teachers as persons and as teachers, on which to rest their education for abiding values. Here they are:

The Bible—the Books of Genesis, Exodus, Isaias, Job, the
    Psalms from the Old Testament; the Four Gospels
    and selected Epistles of Saint Paul from the New.
The *Iliad* of Homer
The *Apology* of Plato
The *Aeneid* of Virgil
The *Divine Comedy* of Dante
The Complete Works of Shakespeare

These books possess threefold greatness. They are great and unexcelled in their ideas, their authors, their forms of expression.

God is the greatest of all ideas, the greatest of authors. Under His inspiration, the writers of the Scriptures have transcribed the greatest of all books. The Bible is humanity's text on God in His relation to man and on man in his relation to God, our daily paper to and from eternity. A perennial classic, it has become in the past twenty-five years a best seller in many translations and paraphrases, in serial and celluloid, the greatest story ever told. To speak of the Bible in our vernacular: it is a compendium of great ideas—eternity, infinity, omnipotence, immortality, sin, suffering, justice, atonement, beatitude; a documentary on good and evil, a commercial on eschatology, the four last things: death, judgment, hell, heaven.

As a teacher one can hardly begin his teacher training through reading better than with the Bible. I remember one little boy very reproachfully saying, "I go to the school that don't give God to the kids." The teacher who reads the world's greatest classic, through his own being, gives God to the kids, let legislation be whatever it may be.

The *Iliad* is the second of our great books for teacher education. I should like also to include the *Odyssey*. Both epics are so timely in this age of world wars, world travel, international exchanges. Both are set against canvasses as spectacular as our most majestic moving pictures, such as *Ben Hur, Caesar and Cleopatra*. Both are laid in lands as controversial today as they were in Homer's time. They are epics of love and jealousy and hate, rivalry and revenge, beauty and its many betrayals, the final fidelity of mothers and wives. Again here are worlds of great ideas, of human beings, in the singing tongue of our greatest epic poet.

In his *Apology*, Plato presents in Socratic dialogue and monologue the inscrutable problems of death and immortality, questions that tease us out of thought as persistent and mysterious to each one of us as they were to Socrates and his disciples. Teacher education can include few lessons more abiding than the *Apology.*

We come to Virgil's *Aeneid.* Historians tell us that at a time more like our own than any in the past, Virgil changed the minds of Rome. He wrote of arms and a hero, indeed, a survivor of world war, a D.P. seeking a home and freedom. His only army was an aged father, a wife, a child. His journey took him through the dark regions of Hades to the spacious plains of Elysium, the only immortality that his paganism knew. The *Aeneid* is a classic protest against war. What teacher cannot read it for its timeless values today?

The *Divine Comedy* takes one on the same journey, part way with Virgil, to the ecstatic end with the fourteenth century Christian poet, Dante. "In the middle of the journey of our life," he writes, "I came to myself in a dark wood where the straight way was lost. So bitter is it that scarcely more is death." Out of it he was led by human wisdom to the depths of Hell, by divine Wisdom to paradise, to the Beatific Vision. Here again for the education of our teachers are abiding, everlasting values in the language of perfect poetry.

As a young teacher, trying to educate myself while meeting a full schedule of high school classes, I read one play of Shakespeare a day until I had figuratively swallowed them all. I shall never forget the experience. I recommend it unconditionally to those here as partially educated as myself. Having recommended it I shall not try to describe its richness and magnitude. I trust that you will find them out for yourselves if you do not already know them.

As a proof of the values of this Shakespeare omnibus let me say that whenever I find myself marooned in a hospital or a hotel or even a convention, I lose myself in a volume of Shakespeare, open at any play, and am immersed in intellectual beatitude until I am jolted back to today by the ubiquitous public address system or a wrist watch.

As yet, we have said no word about technical training, professional preparation, nor shall we. We have laid out a world map of the greatest of natural and supernatural ideas. We invite our young teachers to a life of map-traveling among these and other great ideas. This they can do through reading with penetration and judgment: penetration that is honest and profound, judgment that is honest and courageous. This they can do, too, without conflict with required courses.

A program of great books such as here suggested may well substitute for some of the repetitious courses in methods without content with which our schools of education are unfortunately bogged down. Such a program leads us to the world's greatest ideas, recorded for us by the world's greatest authors.

We have not adverted to the fact that these books also acquaint us with the world's greatest areas and forms of literary expression. The Bible is a library in itself, of history, philosophy, poetry, narrative, chronology, theology. Plato is a text on philosophy. Homer and Virgil are classics in epic poetry. Dante is our supreme Christian poet. Shakespeare is poet, philosopher, apologist, dramatist. We are inviting our teachers in their education to transcendent and lasting values. These can hardly fail to evoke the young teacher's capacity as a person. They can hardly fail to reflect their influence on her as a teacher.

No doubt most of us older teachers have mental shelves of the books that we can least afford not to know. Such a shelf is constantly and conservatively added to as one after the other of the reserve volumes is completed. This easily provides rich intellectual growth and enjoyment for a lifetime.

Parenthetically, may I interject that all the great books

I have listed, with the single exception of Shakespeare, were Chaucer's bedtime reading.

We cannot know books without knowing languages. The plural is important. Languages are keys. They open doors to worlds of wonder, more easily reached than Mars or the moon. Our own English language—or American-English—is among the newest doors. It admits us to only a very modern world. There are the classical keys, Greek and Latin particularly. They open into cultures of an ancient past. Our best secondary schools still keep these doors ajar. Our most distinguished scholars are still our classicists. Whatever our substitutes for Greek and Latin in our liberal arts training, they are substitutes.

We Americans suffer from a national speech impediment. We are a tongue-tied people. We speak only one language, and that in a pretty makeshift way. Take away our slogans and our slang and where would most of us be?

Now is the acceptable time to learn to use our own language beautifully, to learn to read and to speak other modern languages with some ease. I shall not forget coming upon a French boy of ten, at his home in a suburb of Paris, teaching himself English with victrola records. I shall not forget Clare Boothe Luce, teaching herself Spanish in the same way, and more recently Italian. Our young teachers may very well join such goodly company.

Let us put keys into the hands of our young teachers, keys to our modern if not our ancient worlds. Not until they have opened these doors with some courage and assurance will they realize the joy of such possession. I could suggest their subscribing to at least one foreign-language magazine as homework, reading it aloud if possible. A foreign edition of *Reader's Digest* might be excellent for a beginning.

However unprofessional we have been up to this moment, we shall seem to shed even the gestures of professionalism now. We are returning to even more abiding values than books and languages. We are concerning ourselves with life. Life is almost completely omitted in our studies in education.

Years ago I read in Robert Louis Stevenson this uncompromising statement: "Books are a mighty bloodless substitute for life." Life for him meant the out-of-doors, skies, trees, mountains, the world of nature, travels with a donkey, a night among the pines. Franz Werfel, in his *Song of Bernadette,* reproached the citizens of the little French village with their flagrant obtuseness to the obvious. He wrote impatiently: "Your pedestrian minds are unaware of the universe." He, too, had in mind the phenomenal world that belongs to all of us. The mere effort of looking and listening, tasting, touching attentively, reverently the particular locus in the universe in which we happen to be lifts us out of mediocrity, makes us a little less than the angels.

I would ask a knowledge and a love of the universe as an abiding value in education. This can begin very simply with wild flowers, birds, trees. I think of a convocation, given by a college president, on the subject, "Weeds." Students quoted it for years, a rather good record for a convocation. I remember mountain hikes with college students in quest of fritillaries, pentstemon, lungwort. In Indiana we know the day, and the hour almost, for the first hepatica and the last fringed gentian.

How many of our young teachers can take their classes through the seasons in terms of the changing natural life about them? All this, by way of conversation, recreation, or even hobby, a category which I deplore.

Yet this is a richer, more unforgettable experience than one finds in libraries or professional books on education. These are strangely silent on the great book of the universe as a basic text. Some teachers do know it, however, and do study it.

Some time ago I found myself seated next to the vice

president of the University of Minnesota at a North Central Association luncheon. We might have been at a loss for a satisfactory subject of conversation. Our second sentence, however, took us into the world of wild birds. From then on the luncheon did not matter. I have forgotten all about the theme of the convention and its speakers. I shall never forget how my good neighbor explained that by cutting an orange in half and setting it open-face up on a pointed stick in the garden I could attract flocks of evening grosbeaks to our campus.

Anne Lindbergh has shared with us her contemplative world of oceans and ocean shores, her *Gift from the Sea*. We cannot mistake the "Primeval rhythms of the sea-shore. Rollers on the beach, wind in the pines, the slow flapping of herons across the dunes. . . . One falls under their spell, relaxes, stretches out prone. One becomes, in fact, like the element on which one lies, flattened by the sea; bare, open, empty as the beach. . . . One never knows what chance treasures these easy unconscious rollers may toss up, on the smooth white sand of the conscious mind."

The lessons, the teachers are very old. Job knew them well, and David did. Need we cite the Greeks, the Romans, the medieval encyclopedias, Chaucer with his catalogue of trees, his parliament of fowls? Above all, need we cite the New Testament, its parables by which Jesus lifted the world of natural being to similitudes of the kingdom of heaven?

Within the past month a young college graduate came into my office. She had just returned from two years with the Red Cross in northern Africa and Germany. She had been described to me as a girl full of "zip," not the type of person to whom I might have looked for a Great Books devotee, or a bird watcher. She had learned "kitchen French" but little German in the American unit where she was stationed, so she had made some beginning of this unacademic program that I cherish. But she said to me with almost pathetic insistence: "Teach your students to be resourceful. Tell them how to interest themselves in others. Show them how to put their time to some decent use." She continued: "I have been with young service men who have only two ideas of diversion: radio and movies. These failing, they are helpless."

At once the universe came to my mind. Why not study the stars? Chaucer had written *The Astrolabe,* a child's book of stars for his ten-year-old son, little Lewis—a model on the art of teaching and the discipline of learning, the quadrivium particularly. He had written for the youth—the "yonge, fresshe folkes" of his day—on birds, trees, the countryside, the seasonal recreations. My young friend's servicemen had swallowed this universe like a pill and it hadn't given them even a twinge of indigestion.

These boys are not only in Europe. They are everywhere. They are not all boys either. A great many are young women. A great many are teachers.

There are ways and ways of studying the Great Books, of acquiring in part at least a modern language or two. But who will teach our younger grownups the difference between a sycamore, a bird, and a goldfinch? Beautiful books abound. Audiovisual aids and all the wonder worlds of heaven and earth and ocean are easily available. Our elementary textbooks are fascinating. I can easily imagine the candidate for a B.S. in education taking possession of her small brother's books of knowledge as the big brother takes possession of his electric train. But better than all, we have the world itself to look at and learn and love; this world "so full of a number of things, I'm sure we should all be as happy as kings."

If we knew and loved our world and our universe as we should, atomic destruction would be unthinkable.

Our young teachers may not find all the best values in education even in the best books on education. I have before me Arthur Bestor's uncompromising *Educational Waste-*

lands; Gilbert Highet's *Art of Teaching;* Sir Richard Livingstone's two great studies on education. I have read and thought much on their wisdom, as have you. I prize these classics of our profession.

Some time ago I was returning from Seattle. We were crossing the majestic northern Rockies in a snowstorm. As I looked out over the great immensities of mountain peak and snow a bald eagle swept into view, descended slowly and settled on a great naked branch of a fire-blackened pine. Perhaps no one in all the world saw this lone king on his stark throne except myself. Perhaps I have no sense of values. But for me this is one of the great moments of my life, one with which Bestor, or Highet, or Livingstone cannot compete. We find our great teachers and our great lessons everywhere, even from a train window.

As students our young teachers can influence one another by the enthusiasm, vitality, frankness, and courage of their conversations. Taking only a moment for this subject let us propose for discussion among themselves any one of the many ideas suggested by our brief list of great books, of languages, of life. The results will be rich and unforgettable.

Apart from the influence of their teachers and fellow students our teacher education must provide abiding values in subjects studied. My recommendations may seem to fall under categories of literature and languages. Other and even richer areas await in history, philosophy, theology. The fine arts, the sciences are worlds in themselves. Our common quest is the promised land of legitimate knowledge. We all ask the question that one small boy put to his very scholarly father: "When will I know as much as I don't know?"

The subject about which students are seeking knowledge most eagerly now is a religion "based on God as a Supreme Being." An average student from Bowdoin College when asked if he thought theology was the queen of sciences said: "I don't know, but I can see how it could be." Twenty or thirty years ago the question would probably have been dismissed as nonsense.

Perhaps the teaching of youth is itself the most abiding of all values in teacher education. If that is so, and I suspect that it is, with what alacrity our labor of learning is transmuted into a labor of love.

XVI

Conversations with Children

The Twins

THEY stood on my threshold, Rebecca and Rachel, seven
years old, twins as unlike in appearance as Esau and Jacob
might have been at their age. Eagerly I welcomed them into
my little world.

This means my office, two fairly small rooms, really, like
two halves of a walnut shell, with a connecting door. I often
call this home of mine a nutshell. Against the walnut-stained
birchwood door of the inner room hangs a small crucifix,
a flat silhouette in buffed copper. A frieze of prints lines the
wainscoted walls, a Fra Angelico, vertical figures from
Chartres, manuscripts predating Columbus, a picture of
Father Lebbe, a Belgian missioner to China, that no one
ever forgets. On the mantel are an old, old ivory chalice,
carved into veritable lacework, and an angel of Venetian
glass. One side of the doorway may astound you with its
great picture of Noah's ark; the other with the sequel, the
ship of the Church and a net like a patchwork quilt cast
into the sea. Both are by Norman Laliberte in one of his
most graphic manners. A Buddha, maps of London, Oxford,
Paris; a globe, books, and a quaint collection of canes find
their proper places on shelves and wall spaces.

The outer room surrenders itself to administration, to books, files, a desk. One wall holds a memorable fresco of Mary Magdalen, reminiscent in its pale pastel, of the catacombs. The bookcases are topped by a diptych of Bonfigli, Chinese cloisonné bowls, a grim German polychromed wood carving of Don Quixote, two black ivory elephants. An interesting stylized balsawood statue of Mary Magdalen keeps them company. A Florentine Madonna with Child, in wood, polychromed, mothers them all. On this particular morning tuberous begonias in a flat bowl made a spot of wonder on the desk. Stephen Loechner's "Madonna of the Rose Garden" looked down from the wall in approval.

The twins ventured in. Rebecca needed no induction into the amenities of administration. She promptly settled herself in the biggest chair in the inner room and gave herself up to considering her new environment. The globe on the window sill was a big enough world for her.

Rachel lost and thoughtfully tried to find herself in terms of each of many things in the two rooms. A delicate vase from Venice interested her. She looked at a book of good prints with no question, no word of comment. She regarded Don Quixote with discernment as I put the little wooden dreamer in her hands. Saint Mary Magdalen, cut from balsawood, she held carefully in her arms. We were speaking in silences, mostly. At last, looking slowly around, she said, "Everything here has been made into something beautiful." With what vision does this child look out on the world!

Presently she went back with Rebecca to their mother, taking with her the most beautiful thing of all.

Freddie

Freddie's father brought him to meet me one evening after dinner. He left us to our own conversational devices. Freddie was nine. We had no difficulty in reconciling the discrepancy in our ages.

We looked at books. We looked at a great assortment of canes, walking sticks from all over the world. Finally we came to an odd assortment of bells. They had been gathered quite unintentionally on my bookshelves, but, like the canes, spoke of United Nations in their proper tintinnabulary language. Freddie and I rang elephant bells, big and small, from India, a delicate slender bell from Vietnam, a rough sheep bell from Vermont. A pretty enameled bell on the mantel disappointed our expectations in its half-hearted response to our ringing. We recaptured something of the California Franciscan missions in bells from San Francisco, San Carlos, San Juan Capistrano, San Luis Obispo.

Finally we came to a little rough cast bell, unpolished, and with a crude piece of metal hung by a wire for a tongue. But this was the sweetest-toned of all.

"This bell came from Nazareth," I told my young guest. "Do you know of anyone who ever lived in Nazareth?"

He puzzled a bit and then looked up brightly. "Did you?" he asked.

"No, Freddie," I answered. "I have been in Nazareth but have never lived there. There was a little boy once like you—Jesus, who grew up there."

"Oh, yes," came the quick reply. "Then He got to be a teacher and then they killed Him."

Without expanding this capsule biography of Christ, I asked, "Why did Jesus let men kill Him, Freddie?"

This question required more deliberation. Finally, the thoughtful answer came, "Because He did not know a better way of taking us to heaven. He gives us a better chance than we give Him." To which commentators have little to add.

Outer Space

The elevator stopped. I stepped out at the fifth floor waiting room of the clinic to which I had come. A handsome little boy of perhaps five was established in the settee facing

me, absorbed in his pad and pencil. I walked over to him
and asked: "Are you doing homework?"

"Not homework," he answered. "I'm drawing."

"Oh, I see," I said, properly rebuffed.

Putting pad and pencil in my hand, he challenged: "Can
you draw a star?"

"Yes, I can draw a star," I answered, and produced one
with alacrity.

He took back his tools and proceeded to draw two tri-
angles, not properly juxtaposed. Ignoring the lack of co-
ordination, I said: "I see you have drawn Solomon's star.
I drew the star of David." This he did not follow but went
on working with his chubby left hand.

I found a chair on the other side of the room and began
to read. Presently my small friend was beside me on his
artist quest.

"Can you draw an airplane?" he asked.

"No, I'm afraid I can't," I admitted.

"Can you draw a helicopter?"

"No, I can't draw that either, but I am sure that you can."

This sent him back to his settee. But he soon returned
with his mission accomplished.

"This is a heavy freight helicopter," he explained. "It
carries great cargoes to Africa and California and far-distant
countries." His text was a great compliment to the television
programs he had listened to.

"This helicopter could hardly carry an automobile, could
it?" I asked.

"Oh, yes; it's thirty feet long," he informed me.

Then as we looked down the corridor about thirty feet
we agreed that several cars could fit into that area. Mean-
while, three small wobbly circles had appeared on the paper.

"These are Jupiter and Mars and the earth," he told me.

"Have you seen the moons of Jupiter?" I asked.

"Some of them," he answered a bit uncertainly.

"And the rings of Saturn?"

"No, I don't know that," with certainty.

Pointing to a little tail attached to the earth, he explained that this was the means by which the earth contacted the other planets. "They are in outer space," he announced triumphantly.

"When you are a man, do you think that you will go into outer space?" I ventured.

"It's cold out there," he recoiled. "But not Mars. Mars is hot."

Then I asked my favorite question.

"How far can you see?"

He didn't know.

"Can you see a man a mile away?"

"Perhaps."

"Two miles away?"

He doubted it.

"But you can see the sun."

"Oh, yes."

"The sun is ninety million miles away and even then we cannot bear to look straight at it."

He wrote down the figures, 90, then added three zeros. The thousands he knew. Three more zeros made the millions, which were his great new discovery.

Just then his parents came out of the doctor's office. In excitement he ran to them.

"She talked to me about outer space," he said in delight, "and the sun is ninety million miles from the earth."

As he waved goodbye from the elevator I realized that I had ventured into a world far beyond outer space.

XVII

The Catholic College Changes Its Mind

EDUCATION is possibly the most important, the most inclusive problem before the American people today. We are all familiar with its articulations: enrollment, teachers, federal aid; foundation, corporation, personal aids; desegregation. Solutions are not easy, are not simple. They will not be arrived at, completely and entirely, in this political administration, or the next. But they can be solved sanely and intelligently. If this were not so, why should we labor the question of education? The subject itself should teach us the answers, should point to basic prudent solutions. Humanity is not in its infancy that has no past to which to look for direction. It is not bereft of experience, with no history from which to read recurrent patterns, causes, effects, wise and foolish; temperate and arrogant courses of human conduct in nations, in individuals exercising brief temporal domination. The future of education, Christian education, in America is set against the horizon of the second millennium of the Christian era. Only those of us in school now can anticipate being present for this big birthday.

We who can look back forty years can make some prognosis of the magnitudes of changes if survivals through the past four decades can be any measure at all. Let us look at three profiles, dated 1920 to 1961:

Profile one—our country: the flaming twenties, depression, World War II, the iron curtain and its implications.

Profile two—our colleges: accreditation, the elective system, standardization, the democratic idea with progressive education as its exponent, priorities for science, language laboratories, the peace corps, airborne education.

Profile three—the world: airways for travel, communication, exploration, nuclear fission, the bomb, the satellite, outer space, emerging underdeveloped continents on our own planet.

Numbers may prove nothing beyond my curiosity in making these summaries. They can serve as a starting point from which I, at least, can look forty years ahead to the year 2,000. That, I believe, at our present tempo, is quite far enough. Values change too rapidly to be significant beyond that.

We are not without distinguished educators who predict that no more than ten of the hundred and more women's colleges now in existence will be functioning in 2061. They report that the faculties, deans, and presidents of these colleges would wish their schools to survive essentially as they are today. All this is possible. I think it is neither necessary nor inevitable. Speaking for the Catholic college for women, I think that it will not happen.

My first reason is that the Catholic college changed its mind to meet the exigencies of the past forty years, even of every past year, and will change it to meet present and future demands, contingencies, emergencies. This involves no change in principles, in objectives. It concerns adaptations of methods to current needs in applying principles for the achievement of its purposes.

The college is always educating youth. This is one basic constant; others we will refer to later. This education is always contemporary. It meets the needs of the current generation with the current facilities. All good colleges do this. The Catholic college builds this adaptable curriculum upon a body of unchanging truth, theological and philosophical. It is not pragmatic. In this it differs from much of our college education today.

The Catholic college for women is operated by sisters, religious women living under a rule of life and evangelical vows. Their rule and manner of life dedicate them to a profession of perfection as exacting in its nature as the religious life is in its character. So you find the sisters receiving this preparation at the best graduate schools here and abroad. Our own faculty hold Doctors' degrees from the universities of California, Columbia, Harvard, Yale, Notre Dame, and the Catholic University to name only some of many. You find sisters receiving Guggenheim Fellowships, Fulbright Scholarships, National Science Awards. You find sisters professionally prepared, lecturing reverently to a younger generation of sister-teachers on the birth of a baby, on psychiatry, on the civic duty of intelligent voting.

The sister on a college faculty today may be an artist, a concert pianist, an author, a poet. Hers may be the one-woman show of modern sculpture that is attracting such surprised and enthusiastic comments among exacting critics. She may be the recipient of a government grant to continue her anthropological studies of a particular primitive Indian tribe in South America. She may be a research student in cancer, lecturing to clinics and larger audiences in some of our great medical centers.

The sister may even have brought into being the graduate programs in theology for sisters and other laywomen, enabling them to earn Doctors' degrees in theology and Sacred Scripture. No such opportunities are as yet available in the United States for laymen.

Out of a brochure, "The Education of Sister Lucy," published by one of our colleges for women, has grown the Sister-

Formation Movement. Through generous foundation grants a small group of well qualified sisters have set up the basic professional structure for the training of the religious teacher. Another grant has enabled a sister to spend a year in Europe observing conditions and opportunities available there for the academic perfecting of the sister for her life as a college teacher.

These are only some of the ways in which the Catholic college keeps changing its mind, perfecting and adapting it to generation after generation. There are other less serious, even humorous ways. Who is surprised now to see a sister driving a station wagon, a sister being interviewed on a TV program, a sister on a panel with a group of professors at a National Educational Convention?

Minds have been changed on that most sacred of conventions, the religious habit, for reasons of safety, economy, comfort, and congruity. And who shall explain the change of attitude that has made the nun the darling of the stage, the motion picture, the best seller?

I have questioned professionals in all of these matters and have received this answer. Perhaps it is the general desire of the public today for the preservation of dignity and convention in our slipshod abandonment of these. Perhaps also it is the element of quaint and innocent humor in the archaisms of the nun's habit, her somewhat patterned propriety of speech and conduct in social life. At any rate, it is something which no other women in all the world can contribute to the common life and the common good.

A body of women possessing both such stability and such adaptability is not likely to be destroyed by any intransigencies attributed to it or by its helplessness to survive the civilizations of the future.

A second reason for survival is the genius of the religious community itself which operates the Catholic college, its quality of corporate permanence, the life investment of every member for God's sake and her total service to His world. A body so humanly selfless, so supernaturally motivated has no Achilles' heel vulnerable to fatal human attack or temporal destruction. Moreover, its almost mercurial adaptability is possible only in terms of an absolute stability of faith and hope and love, of theology and philosophy by which to measure, to evaluate, and to accept change. Lacking these, the Catholic college would be like the man who to fasten his boat to the shore of a river pounded a nail to the prow and tied his rope to the nail.

My third reason for believing in the survival of the Catholic college for women is that it educates them on two levels, the natural and the supernatural. It educates them for mortality and immortality, for time and eternity. It teaches the student as a rational animal and as a child of God. These are the hurdles that few other educational systems take unambiguously, unfalteringly, and unalterably. They offer answers and hopes for which every human being clamors, even while rejecting or refusing them. I am reminded of the little boy who said of his experience indignantly, "I go to the school that don't give God to the kids."

How will a Catholic college educate young women of tomorrow? How prepare them for the millennium? How save themselves from a possible decline and fall? With Millicent McIntosh, the president of Barnard College, I should say by a wisely revised curriculum restoring history as history to a place of proper eminence, by making more than one modern language an actual acquirement; by regarding the student as a human being and, better, as a child of God; by making the college a lived life, an initiation into the great business of being a responsible, active citizen of a community, a country, a world. Most of all, I should present a college education, the entire experience of the intellectual life and academic development, as an investment in immortality.

With Jacques Barzun, I should be very practical in regarding economies to be applied day in, day out, as to the use of the educational plant facilities, the economy of faculty time and student ability. I should open the doors and windows to all the world, inviting and encouraging students to enter into its many great promised lands, to know and to love their inhabitants.

Then, I should recall the counsel of Gamaliel: "If this work is of men it will be overthrown. But if it is of God you will not be able to overthrow it; else perhaps you may find yourselves fighting even against God."

I should repeat the frightening rhetorical question of God Himself: "When the Son of Man comes, will He find, think you, faith on earth?" Let that be the year 2000. Let it be 2061. Our answer is and always will be "Yes." About this the Catholic college does not change its mind.

You may think that my case for the Catholic college rests on the fact that it is in a sense tied to God's apron strings. That is true. It is also true that our present epidemic of contraception will have prevented the lives of many more possible non-Catholic than Catholic students for the years 1985 and beyond. Also, I am not ignoring the fact that the law of average mortality among all small colleges will continue to operate. I have no doubt about the fact and the nature of difficult days ahead, a very fight for survival. Even so, I think of these lines out of Browning:

"Sudden the worst turns the best to the brave . . ."

and

"I was ever a fighter, so—one fight more."

Our Catholic colleges, indeed all our private, Christian colleges have the will and the courage to fight for their lives. They are the brave. The basic qualities of all education, love of wisdom and truth, the integrity of the mind, honesty in its training and its use, respect for authority and its representatives, reverence for the dignities of the human being and the sacredness of life itself, all these derive from our private, Christian, Church-related colleges. All of these are of their essence. They may be assumed but are not necessarily sponsored by our tax-supported schools.

We have not properly assessed our private schools for what they are, what we owe them, what only they as colleges are free to teach us. When we do this, we will not repudiate these wise, intrepid, truly Catholic mothers of our minds.

XVIII

Dame Julian of Norwich

You may have met her face to face in *The Man on a Donkey,* a contemporary novel by H. F. M. Prescott. You may have discovered her fugitive presence in the third of T. S. Eliot's *Four Quartets.* You may have found her spiritual insight matched by the most delicately intuitive passages of Antoine de Saint-Exupéry's *The Little Prince.* Years ago you could have known her as the original of the recluse in *The Anchorhold* by Enid Dinnis. She has been fairly persistent, this fourteenth century contemplative, Dame Julian of Norwich.

Despite the fact that she can be identified by nothing beyond a place name, she may be the best known, best loved, most simply articulate of the early English mystics. This does not mean that she is well or widely known in her own country or even in her own city.

Shortly after noon one bright day in early July we drove into the Cathedral close of Norwich. We had gone to ask the rector to direct us to the site of the former home of Dame Julian. According to our best information (and entirely correct) it had been a little anchorhold or one-room dwelling outside the Church of Saint Julian. The rector had never heard of blessed Julian and knew only vaguely of the church which had given her its name. He suggested that we drive down into the town and make inquiry from some of the folk there. We did.

Near the fishing wharves a half dozen wind-blown sailors told us that a bit up the road we would come to Julian's alley. A sharp turn up the hill to the right would bring us to Saint Julian's Church. In five minutes we were there.

The church, built of field stone, very small, sturdy, clings to the side of a determined little hill and faces west. Even the experienced Roman Catholic could be misled by the tabernacle with its veil, the sanctuary lamp, the stations of the cross, the statue of the Curé of Ars. But the caretaker, a woman, was quick to obviate our incipient error. The shrine of Dame Julian is now under high Anglican protection.

This shrine we found on the sunny south side of the church. Here, in a small room or anchorage a rarely gifted gentlewoman lived for many years during the fourteenth and well into the fifteenth century. Here she spent her days in prayer, meditation, and contemplation. Here, probably in 1373, she experienced from four o'clock one morning until the following night sixteen "shewings" of the Passion of Jesus Christ and the immediately-related mysteries, known to us now as the *Revelations of Divine Love*. No vestige of the little cell remains. Against the church wall, however, a beautifully congruous marker preserves the identity of the spot for pilgrims who, like ourselves, come in love to the earthly home of one of the dearest of English mystics.

A simple pediment about two feet high and four feet long carries, in fine Roman incised letters, this text:

> Here Dwelt Mother Julian
> Anchoress of Norwich c. 1342–1430
> "Thou art enough to me."

On the pediment rests a perpendicular Carrara marble slab, excellently proportioned, and plain, except for a crucifix in high relief. The ground at the base of the crucifix says merely,

"Lo, how I love Thee."

Six hundred years, nineteen hundred years quietly lost themselves that sunny afternoon in the presence of this commentary on all life and all love. We had found Dame Julian in her essential milieu, her basic world of contemplation. Presently we were conscious of pink rambler roses growing at a discreet distance in bright, untroubled profusion. Nothing could have been less studied, more right. We walked away, sharing with Dame Julian this outward sign of the Thomas à Kempis text, "In the cross is joy of spirit." [1]

Time and research will probably add nothing to what we already know of this gentle woman. This comes to us in her own words, from her single book, a spiritual autobiography of the most absolute type, and from a few scattered facts and conjectures that have survived with it. From these her best critics conclude that she was probably a Norfolk or a Yorkshire woman of refined breeding and education. She was born in 1343 and was still alive in 1442. Her book she wrote fifteen years after the experiences which it records. One sixteenth century manuscript survives in the British Museum. The Bibliothèque Nationale possesses the only other, a seventeenth century manuscript. The East Midland dialect of the texts may indicate the native countryside of the author. The earliest printed edition, by the Benedictine monk Serenus de Cressy in 1670, supports the opinion that Dame Julian was herself a Benedictine nun or oblate. Neither her family name nor her religious name survives. Her sole identification comes

[1] Saint Julian's Church was destroyed in an air raid in 1942, but is now restored.

from the little Church of Saint Julian that sheltered her. She
is Dame Julian of Norwich. Later feminization of the name
to Juliana has added nothing except the sign of the times
from which it sprang.

Mysticism had come to full flower during her lifetime.
Richard Rolle's *Fire of Love* was current reading among the
literate. Abundant surviving manuscripts attest to its wide
circulation. The anonymous *Cloud of Unknowing* became
a text for spiritual adepts. Walter Hilton offered direction to
pedestrians in perfection. Perfection itself, the spiritual life,
its rich preternatural and supernatural possibilities were
known and understood for what they are, an experimental
knowledge of God and the great realities of existence. The
more logical and courageous one was, the more readily he
set about measuring up to these.

Spirituality, being bounded only by God, offers wide choices
to its disciples. One finds that they made full use of this
latitude. One would choose the complete subordination of
himself to the will of God as his path to perfection. One gave
himself to the burning ardors of divine love. Dame Julian
dedicated herself to the passion of Christ in close, sharp focus,
with the blocking out of all but the fewest details. For instance, apart from the crucifix in her room, she does not speak
of the cross on which Christ died, the nails, the lance that
pierced His side, although she describes the wound as "a fair
delectable place, large enough for all mankind." She makes
no mention of the executioners, the noonday darkness, the
quaking of the earth. Even as a mystic of the passion, she is
exclusive in her eclecticism, devoting her attention to the
participation of the Blessed Trinity in this divine comedy
rather than to man's physical activity in it. That participation she sees as a "fullhead of joy" and enigmatically "a deed,
the which the blissedful Trinity shall do in the last day, as to
my sight: and what the deed shall be, and how it shall be done,

it is unknown of all creatures which are beneath Christ, and shall be till when it shall be done."

Her revelation of the passion, her participation in it becomes, as she grows in understanding, a revelation of love. Her sufferings, her ecstasy, her shewings have only one meaning. That meaning is love.

With mathematical directness and precision Dame Julian begins her book: "This is a Revelation of Love, that Jesus Christ our endless blisse made in XVI shewings: . . . This Revelation was made to a simple creature unlettered, living in deadlie flesh, the year of our Lord, a thousand three hundred seventy-three, the eighth daie of Maie." Immediately she explains the occasion of her "shewing." Earlier in her spiritual life she had desired *three* gifts by the grace of God.

"The *first*, was mind of the passion.

The *second*, was bodilie sickness.

The *third*, was to have of God's gift three woundes."

Through the first she hoped to share more closely the devotion of Magdalen and the compassion of our Lady in the passion of Christ; through the second she sought purgation from her faults; through the third the wounds of very contrition, compassion, and longing for God.

"This sickness," she says, "I desired in my youth that I might have it when I were thirtie years old. . . . And when I was thirtie years old and a halfe, God sent me a bodilie sickness." For three days she lay at the point of death and received Extreme Unction on the fourth day. At the week's end her curate was sent for to be present at her death. As he held the crucifix before her the room grew dark and she believed herself to be dying. Then she says, "Sodenlie I saw the red blood running down from under the garland [the crown of thorns], . . . And in the same shewing, sodenlie the Trinitie fulfilled my heart most of joy. . . . For the Trinitie is God.

God is the Trinitie, the Trinitie is our Maker, the Trinitie is our Keeper, the Trinitie is our everlasting Lover."

From the very beginning this extraordinary woman shares with us the theology, the psychology, and the physiology of her absolutely immediate and intuitive experience. She "conceaved trulie and mightilie" that it was God Himself Who gave her this shewing of the crowning with thorns and of the Trinitie, "without any meane." She distinguishes among sense knowledge, natural understanding, faith, and immediate intuition with clinical acuteness. Her interpretations should delight the jaded psychiatrist of our day by their sanity, their sureness.

The sight of the passion, for instance, "I sawe," she says, "in my understanding." And in one of the loveliest of all corollaries:

"He brought our Lady Saint Mary to my understanding; I sawe her ghostelie in bodilie likeness, a simple maiden and a meeke, young of age, a little waxen above a child, in the stature as she was when she conceived.

"Also God shewed me in part the wisdome and the truth of her soule; wherein I understood the reverence beholding that she beheld her God that is her Maker, marvailing with great reverence that He would be born of her that was a simple creture of His making. . . ."

"In this sight I did understand verilie that . . . above her is nothing that is made but the blessed manhood of Christ, as to my sight."

Then follows a part of her first revelation, a passage that to a generation absorbed and frightened by the facts of nuclear fission may be the most significant of all Dame Julian's experiences. She says:

"And in this Christ shewed a little thing, the quantitie of a hasel-nutt, lying in the palme of my hand, as me seemed; and it was as round as a ball. I looked thereon with the eie of my understanding, and thought, 'What may this be?' and it was answered generallie thus:

" 'It is all that is made.' I marvelled how it might last: for me thought it might sodenlie have fallen to naught for litlenes.

"And I was answered in my understanding, 'It lasteth, and ever shall: for God loveth it. And so hath all things being by the love of God.'

"In this little thing I sawe three properties.

"The *first* is, that God made it.

"The *second* is, that God loveth it.

"The *third* is, that God keepeth it."

A cosmology more brief and basic and plausible could scarcely be written. An age of science has yet to wrap and enclose the infinities of its universe in such infinity of love.

Her second revelation shows Dame Julian the fair face of Christ, discolored by His passion, "And after this," she says, "I sawe God in a point." A statement so stark, so startling and unequivocal one scarcely meets outside of Sacred Scriptures. It touches the mystic's intuitive certainty that God is at the center, indeed is the core and center of all being. This is the "point" of which Dame Julian speaks. But what of sin? Although she sees that "He is in all things" she "considered with a soft dread, and thought: *What is sin?* Certainly," she says, "God doeth no sin," and understands intuitively that "sin is no deed," it "hath no part of being." It is a negation, a failure, an emptiness of love. Against the pain of this hard hell she sees God's protective presence in our souls ruling and guiding. Here again she repeats "I sawe God in a point." Evidently, she thinks this shewing of great importance.

Upon this one small chronicle on her brief initiation into the world of contemplation and ecstasy one could write a little library of commentary, touching the body of dogmatic and moral theology. Our purpose is much simpler. First, let us enumerate quickly her remaining thirteen visions. Then, in the light of her own exact interpretation, her rare diction, her style, let us look at this girl, this young woman, this rare mystic who could see God and live. We will find that love, too, is her meaning, and that joy is her manner.

The fourth revealed to her Christ's scourging; the fifth the overcoming of the devil; the sixth the degree of happiness in heaven and man's age there; the seventh our feelings of weal and woe; the eighth the death of Christ; the ninth the joy of the Trinity in our redemption; the tenth the pierced heart of Christ. In the eleventh revelation our Lady appears as the source of our joy; in the twelfth Christ glorified; the thirteenth is the consummation of the Passion; the fourteenth God, the end of our quest; the fifteenth the joy of a faithful soul; the sixteenth God's abiding in our souls.

For fifteen years Dame Julian lived quietly in her anchorage contemplating the mysteries that her brief hours of ecstasy had revealed. The world outside her secluded cell went on. Peasants revolted. Boys from Norfolk marched away to fight a spot in the Hundred Years' War. Chaucer began *The Canterbury Tales*. Perhaps he was writing the lovely story of Little Hugh of Lincoln, buried behind the high altar of the Cathedral not too far north of here. She was untouched by it all. She desired simply and "oftentimes to wit in what was our Lord's meaning: and fifteen year and more, I was answered in ghostly understanding, saying thus: 'What wouldest thou wit thy Lord's meaning in this thing? Wit it well: love was his meaning. Who sheweth it thee? Love. Wherefore sheweth he it thee? For love. Hold thee therein, thou shalt wit more in the same. But thou shalt never wit therein other without end.' Thus was I learned that love is our Lord's meaning." Only then did she begin to write.

God's explanation might well preclude any stumbling com-

mentaries of our own on this very great apocalypse. Yet Julian
herself says that "He will have it known more than it is."
Such promulgation is our purpose.

One does not read past the first page of *Revelations of Love*
without knowing that he is in the presence of a personality,
a technique, a style. A girl who, in her teens probably, asks
God for sickness as a means of spiritual perfection is a person
of courage as well as character. Her other two requests, knowledge and the three wounds of the passion, indicate the same
spiritual valor. The reasons for her requests match these in
clarity and directness. Inevitably she finds herself in the
world of the basic doctrines of Christianity: the Trinity, the
Incarnation, the Redemption, sin, grace, personal immortality. She could scarcely have plotted out for her spiritual enterprises areas more infinitely rich and expansive. She never de-
tours however up any inviting path of popular devotion or
supernatural affectation. The exegesis of her sky-scraping
statement, "I sawe God in a point," she transcribes from her
immediate understanding of the being of God. "See I am
God: See I am in all things: See I do all things: See I never
left my hands of my works, ne never shall without end: See
I lead all thing to the end that I ordaine it to, fro without
beginning, by the same might, wisdom, and love, that I made
it with. How should anything be amiss?" Thus mightily,
wisely, and lovingly was the soul examined in this vision.

Even so immediate a knowledge of God could not divert
her from her own spiritual crucifixion with Christ on the
cross. Here we begin to guess at her stature as a person and
a mystic:

"Thus was I learned to choose Jesu for my heaven, Whom
I saw only in pain at that time. . . . And this hath ever been
a comfort to me, that I chose Jesu to be my heaven by His
grace in all this time of passion and sorrow."

Temptation and the devil have little space, comparatively,

in the chronicle. They are present to all the senses of Dame
Julian. She even suffers one onslaught in a dream. But, as
she says laconically, "God shewed that the fiend is damned."
So far as we know her experience of profound contemplation and ecstatic union occurred only once in her life. She
has left no record of any other. She recovers from the acute
illness which prefaced them and spends the remaining seventy
years of her life reliving their infinities and writing of them.
Although she finds herself helpless for words to match her
brave excursion into the world of absolute Reality, she writes
of it like a Doctor of Theology. Creation, sin, Redemption,
the place of the Trinity in the work of salvation, prayer and
its kinds, self-knowledge, the presence of God in His creation,
Christ in the Church, grace, charity, the great areas of dogmatic and moral theology are the subjects on which this
"simple creature" writes unerringly. Parenthetically she states
that she had no revelation regarding the angels. She knows
only what the clerics told her of them.

Her technique follows the manner of her day, a technique
of definition, enumeration, division. In the bleeding of
Christ's head she understands *six* things; God shows her *three*
degrees of the bliss of heaven, *three* ways of beholding the
passion, *three* joys of Christ in His suffering, *three* kinds of
prayer. All our life, in fact, she says, is *three*. This numerical
clarification of her vision confirms both the vision and her
capacity to identify it with human denominators of thought.
Arabic numerals are, moreover, a quick, disconcerting device
for trying the spirits if they be of God.

The great mystics of Julian's time, in this their golden
age, commonly employed the ladder, the scale, the mirror of
perfection for the framework on which to build their spiritual
structures. The familiar method of the schoolmen was one of
enumeration and division. The present revival of Thomistic
philosophy has familiarized us with this. Dame Julian and
her spiritual directors lived in the days of its fruit-gathering

and could scarcely have originated a better technique to serve her need.

Her style, like that of any artist, is herself infused into a language ready to her use, and a more specialized terminology of her own devising. The direct, monosyllabic brevity and clarity of the texts already quoted characterize her entire book. Let two further examples stand for many: "Our failing is dreadful, our falling is shameful; and our dying is sorrowful." And "Mercy worketh, keeping, suffering, quickening, and healing, and all is of tenderness of love."

More surprising to us in these days of psychological analysis is the vocabulary which this medieval woman achieved for supersensuous, preternatural, and supernatural experiences. Any bona-fide psychologist, psychoanalyst, or psychiatrist today can read Dame Julian with keen understanding, and, I dare say, keener surprise. Here is a fair sample of her hyphenations which precede and excel some of the best of our own: general-man, all-man, nature-goodness, nature-soul, nature-substance, sense-soul, sense-part, oneing. One never finds her at a loss for the precise word for any particular experience however new to her and to her own resources of language. If she doesn't possess the right word, she makes it. And she knows how!

More than all else Dame Julian leaves a spiritual legacy to everyone who can enter into the mystery of love through the mystery of suffering. She understands and shares with her readers the epitomes of the universe in the Passion and Crucifixion of Christ; the intrinsic, solicitous presence of God in all things; the essential necessity of God's attributes, and His essential intimacy with the universe. This brings us the heritage of the metaphysician, the theologian, but in the language of the Pater Noster. One might say in the language of the *Ave Maria* after reading this vision of Mary:

"Our good Lord . . . said, 'Wilt thou see her? . . . I wot well that thou wilt see my blessed Mother: for after myself

she is the highest joy that I might shew thee. . . . Wilt thou
see in her how thou art loved? For thy love I made her so
high, so noble, so worthy.' And Jesus . . . shewed me . . .
her . . . litle and simple; . . . then high and noble and
glorious." This is the lady of the medieval world's delight.
One understands why.

Julian's assurance of Christ's help in temptation holds infinite comfort for readers more fearfully tried than herself.

"He said not, thou shalt not be troubled, thou shalt not
be travelled [tempted], thou shalt not be diseased; but he
said, 'Thou shalt not be overcome.' " One can spend a difficult lifetime leaning hard on such a promise.

In a book as compact and copious as the *Revelations of
Divine Love,* any explanation simpler than the text itself is
practically impossible. One can best exercise a certain eclecticism in selecting passages or doctrines of rare interest. Such
is this exposition of the Blessed Trinity in the fourteenth
revelation:

"In our making God Almighty is our kindly Father. And
God all wisdom is our kindly mother, with the love and the
goodness of the Holy Ghost, which is all one God, one Lord.
And in the knitting, and in the oneing he is our very true
spouse, and we his loved wife, and his fair maiden; with which
he was never displeased, for he saith, 'I loved thee, and thou
lovest me, and our love shall never part in two.' I beheld the
working of all the blessed Trinity." A comparison with our
own knowledge of the Trinity measures somewhat the degree
of divine initiation which Julian enjoyed.

Never more acutely than in these poor approximations to
an appraisal of the recluse of Norwich do we find that in our
end is only our beginning. Dame Julian is a teacher and a
text, a life and a love. Beautifully free from morbid emo-
tionalism, self-consciousness, effort, she is spontaneous, art-
less, frank, competent, clear-headed. She eschews even the
existence of abnormal devotionalism. With profound penetra-

tion and unerring orthodoxy she looks into the face of Mary, upon the crucified Christ, beyond the anthropomorphic, to the Beatific Vision of the Trinity. She takes us with her all the way.

Centuries of mediocre Englishmen went into the making of one Shakespeare. The English-speaking world has produced only one Julian. Too late and too little do we know her. It need not be either. You may not go to Norwich to find her. She is a person to be sought in the quiet, even the holy, the all-alone hours of one's life. Her book is the most exciting of divine detective stories for one's bedside at night. When you come as a guest to our guest anchorhold you will find at your bed's head Dame Julian's *Sixteen Revelations of Divine Love.*